Berkshire Studies in European History

GENERAL EDITORS

RICHARD A. NEWHALL

LAURENCE B. PACKARD

SIDNEY R. PACKARD

Berkshire Studies in European History

Under the Editorship of

Richard A. Newhall
Laurence B. Packard
Sidney R. Packard

THE CRUSADES
RICHARD A. NEWHALL, *Williams College*

EUROPE AND THE CHURCH UNDER IN-
NOCENT III
SIDNEY R. PACKARD, *Smith College*

THE COMMERCIAL REVOLUTION
LAURENCE B. PACKARD, *Amherst College*

THE INDUSTRIAL REVOLUTION
FREDERICK C. DIETZ, *University of Illinois*

GEOGRAPHICAL BASIS OF EUROPEAN
HISTORY
J. K. WRIGHT, *American Geographical Society*

THE ENLIGHTENED DESPOTS
GEOFFREY BRUUN, *New York University*

ORGANIZATION OF MEDIEVAL CHRIS-
TIANITY
SUMMERFIELD BALDWIN

THE AGE OF LOUIS XIV
LAURENCE B. PACKARD, *Amherst College*

THE SECOND HUNDRED YEARS WAR,
1689-1815
ARTHUR H. BUFFINTON, *Williams College*

IMPERIALISM AND NATIONALISM IN
THE FAR EAST
DAVID E. OWEN, *Yale University*

EUROPEAN IMPERIALISM IN AFRICA
HALFORD L. HOSKINS, *Tufts College*

THE BRITISH EMPIRE-COMMONWEALTH
REGINALD G. TROTTER, *Queen's University*

MEDIEVAL SLAVDOM AND THE RISE
OF RUSSIA
FRANK NOWAK, *Boston University*

IMPERIAL SPAIN
EDWARD DWIGHT SALMON, *Amherst College*

THE CHURCH IN THE ROMAN EMPIRE
ERWIN R. GOODENOUGH, *Yale University*

NATIONALISM IN THE BALKANS, 1800-
1930
W. M. GEWEHR, *American University*

IMPERIAL RUSSIA, 1801-1917
M. KARPOVICH, *Harvard University*

THE RUSSIAN REVOLUTION, 1917-1931
GEORGE VERNADSKY, *Yale University*

THE
RUSSIAN REVOLUTION
1917-1931

BY

GEORGE VERNADSKY

RESEARCH ASSOCIATE IN HISTORY IN YALE UNIVERSITY
LECTURER ON HISTORY (1931-1932) IN HARVARD UNIVERSITY

NEW YORK
HENRY HOLT AND COMPANY

PREFACE

The college teacher of general European history is always confronted with the task of finding adequate reading for his classes which is neither too specialized and technical nor too elementary. For many topics, including several of the greatest importance, no such material is at the moment available. Moreover, in too many instances, good reading which undeniably does exist is in the form of a chapter in a larger work and is therefore too expensive for adoption as required reading under normal conditions.

The Berkshire Studies in European History have been planned to meet this situation. The topics selected for treatment are those on which there is no easily accessible reading of appropriate length adequate for the needs of a course in general European history. The authors, all experienced teachers, are in nearly every instance actively engaged in the class room and intimately acquainted with its problems. They will avoid a merely elementary presentation of facts, giving instead an interpretive discussion suited to the more mature point of view of college students.

No pretense is made, of course, that these *Studies* are contributions to historical literature in the scholarly sense. Each author, nevertheless, is sufficiently a specialist in the period of which he writes to be familiar with the sources and to have used the latest scholarly contributions to his subject. In order that those who desire to read further on any topic may have some guidance short bibliographies of works in western European languages are given, with particular attention to books of recent date.

Each *Study* is designed as a week's reading. The division into three approximately equal chapters, many of them self-contained and each suitable for one day's assignment, should make the series as a whole easily adaptable to the present needs of college classes. The editors have attempted at every point to maintain and emphasize this fundamental flexibility.

Maps and diagrams will occasionally be furnished with the text when specially needed but a good historical atlas, such as that of Shepherd, is presupposed throughout.

R. A. N.
L. B. P.
S. R. P.

CONTENTS

CHAPTER   PAGE

I. THE BACKGROUND AND IMMEDIATE CAUSES OF THE RUSSIAN REVOLUTION 3

    RUSSIAN EMPIRE. AREA AND POPULATION . 6

    THE POLITICAL STRUCTURE OF RUSSIA BEFORE THE WAR 10

    POLITICAL PARTIES 13

    INDUSTRY AND LABOR 15

    BANKING, FINANCE AND COMMERCE . . 18

    AGRICULTURE 20

    EDUCATION AND CULTURAL LIFE . . . 22

    CHURCH AND RELIGION 24

    THE FOREIGN POLICY OF IMPERIAL RUSSIA . 25

    RUSSIA IN THE WORLD WAR 29

    INFLUENCE OF THE WAR UPON NATIONAL ECONOMY 31

    THE POLITICAL CONFLICT 33

II. THE MARCH AND THE NOVEMBER REVOLUTIONS OF 1917 37

    THE FORMATION OF THE NEW GOVERNMENT 37

    THE FIRST ASPECT OF THE REVOLUTION . . 41

    THE CONTRADICTIONS OF THE REVOLUTION . 42

    FOREIGN POLICIES OF THE RUSSIAN REVOLUTION 46

    THE DOMESTIC POLICY OF THE PROVISIONAL GOVERNMENT 48

    THE SOVIETS 52

    THE KERENSKY OFFENSIVE AND THE JULY UPRISING 55

CONTENTS

CHAPTER   PAGE

THE KORNILOV REBELLION 57

THE ECONOMIC CRISIS 60

THE BOLSHEVIK ASCENDANCY 61

THE VICTORY OF THE BOLSHEVIKS . . . 63

FIRST STEPS OF THE SOVIET GOVERNMENT . 65

THE DISSOLUTION OF THE ARMY AND THE
BEGINNING OF PEACE PARLEYS . . . 69

THE PARTY STRUGGLE, THE BEGINNING OF
THE TERROR AND THE DISBANDING OF THE
CONSTITUENT ASSEMBLY 70

THE BREST-LITOVSK PEACE 72

III. THE CIVIL WAR AND THE SOVIET
STATE, 1918-1931 75

THE EFFECT OF THE REVOLUTION UPON ECO-
NOMIC AND SOCIAL LIFE 77

THE CIVIL WAR 80

THE COMMUNIST INTERNATIONAL . . . 85

ECONOMIC DECAY AND FAMINE . . . 88

THE NEW ECONOMIC POLICY 90

THE NEP IN FOREIGN AFFAIRS . . . 91

THE SOVIET ADMINISTRATIVE AND JUDICIARY
SYSTEM 93

THE COMMUNIST PARTY 96

CULTURAL LIFE UNDER THE SOVIETS . . 98

NATIONAL MINORITIES UNDER THE SOVIETS . 102

THE RENEWAL OF MILITANT COMMUNISM,
THE FIVE-YEAR PLAN 103

THE ECONOMIC DEVELOPMENT OF SOVIET
RUSSIA DURING THE FIRST YEARS OF THE
FIVE-YEAR PLAN, 1928-1931 109

BIBLIOGRAPHICAL NOTE 119

INDEX 127

THE RUSSIAN REVOLUTION, 1917-1931

CHAPTER I

THE BACKGROUND AND IMMEDIATE CAUSES OF THE RUSSIAN REVOLUTION

WE are obviously too near the event to attempt to estimate the significance in world history of the Russian Revolution, but we are not too near to recognize it as one of those elemental historical upheavals the effects of which are felt far beyond the area in which the initial eruption occurs. The nature of these effects and their extent depend on many factors, of which not the least is the outcome in Russia itself of this attempt to change not merely the structure of the state but the fundamental organization of society. It is significant that this attempt is being made in the vast Eurasian area of old Russia, populous and of enormous potential wealth, whose frontiers march with those of Europe and of Asia, whose people are as varied in their origins as are the products of the land, and whose civilization is of the East as well as of the West. It is significant not merely from the international point of view. The fact remains that whatever the external repercussions have been or may be and regardless of the outside influences that may have contributed to bring it about, it is after all a Russian Revolution, one of the great turning points in Russian history. It is in this light, chiefly, that the Revolution will be considered here.

The Russian Revolution is a combination of various revolutionary processes. Indeed, we may even say that there is not one revolution in Russia but several, going on simultaneously. In the first place there is a struggle between autocracy and liberalism. In 1905 the autocracy of the Imperial Government received a mortal blow and it was completely destroyed in March 1917. In November 1917, however, there came a new autocracy, the autocracy of the Communist Party. This new autocracy is regarded by some as even more ruthless and unscrupulous than the old one, and there is certainly incomparably less personal freedom in Communist Russia today than existed under the Imperial régime. Consequently, a constant struggle for the elemental rights of the individual is now going on.

Secondly, there is the centuries-long struggle of the Russian peasants for land. In 1861, at the time of their emancipation, the peasants received about one-half of the total area of land then under cultivation; by 1917 on the eve of the Revolution they owned about three-fourths of it. But the peasants' thirst for land was insatiable, and they would support any government without exception which would promise them all of the available land. The Soviet Government satisfied their aspirations and early in 1918 the peasants divided all the land among themselves. But then the Government which had given them land, began to take their products away from them. The peasants then tried to rise against the Government; this peasant movement was a very important phase of the Civil War. Finally, Lenin, the first Red dictator, was obliged to come to an agreement with the peasants and he promised them that he would not interfere with their right to dispose of the products of their farms. This agreement was the so-called NEP,[1] and was in force until the end of 1927, at which time, Stalin, the next Red dictator, began a new offensive against the peasants. Stalin tried to compel them to leave their individual farms for the collective farms. This brought a new wave of discontent and the problem is not yet solved.

Another revolution going on in Russia is cultural, and is a result of the existence of sharp contradictions between the mentality of the educated classes and the uneducated or half-educated masses. Although the Revolution dispersed the former educated élite, the masses are now trying to raise their own common cultural level. In addition, there is a serious religious crisis. Before the Revolution the non-conformists were oppressed by the official Eastern, or Greek, Orthodox Church. At the present time both the Orthodox Church and the other religious denominations must defend themselves against the implacable pressure of official atheism. The cultural revolution is further aggravated by the question of national minorities, each of which claims an educational system of its own; several of these minority groups also have peculiar religious problems.

Another, and perhaps the most important, revolution in Russia is the Industrial Revolution. Its progress was furthered by the administration of Witte in the last decade of the nineteenth century. A period of depression followed. About 1907 industrial development began again and continued up to the outbreak of the World War, and even during the war until 1916,

[1] *New Economic Policy.* See below, p. 90.

although progress was slower in that period. Following 1917 there came the industrial break-down of the first years of Revolution and Civil War; then came the reconstructive stage of the so-called NEP period. In 1928 forced and rapid industrialization began under the five-year plan. It is impossible at this time to foretell the results of this latest policy. Naturally, this Industrial Revolution produced a considerable proletariat which is still increasing in number. Since for various historical reasons the labor movement in Russia was not molded by moderate socialists, as in Germany, but by the extremists of the Bolshevik or Communist Party which is the Russian form of Social Democracy, it is not surprising that the Communist Party has finally succeeded in establishing a real dictatorship over Russian Labor and the Russian people.

Although in its earlier stages—in 1905 and in March, 1917—the Russian Revolution may be compared either with the French Revolution of 1789 or with the European Revolutions of 1848, the later Communist stage in Russia is a factor unique in history of which even the Paris Commune of 1870 is but a feeble prototype.

RUSSIAN EMPIRE. AREA AND POPULATION

To represent the Russian Empire before the Revolution as moribund is to consider only the serious defects in its organization and to ignore the vital forces which it unquestionably possessed. That these vital forces could be called into action was particularly noticeable after the violent shock of the year 1905—the first stage of the Revolution. It is true, however, that the action of these vital forces was restricted by historical conditions which were more favorable to revolutionary than to evolutionary processes. In the first place, the general progress of the Russian people was delayed by the political reaction which, with brief intervals, had been protracted through the whole of the nineteenth and the beginning of the twentieth centuries. Secondly, progress in the different spheres of Russian life was uneven. Thus, while the political organization of the Empire was antiquated and cumbersome, industrial development since the last decade of the nineteenth century was amazingly rapid. An unevenness of development no less striking characterized the different regions and peoples of the Empire.

Before the World War the Russian Empire controlled an immense territory, nearly equal in size to that of the British Empire. But unlike the British Empire, which includes various territories scattered over the five parts of the world, Russia was a compact *bloc* enclosed within continuous borders. However, there were just as great differences between the various parts of the Russian Empire as there are between the different parts of the British Empire. Let us imagine Great Britain, Canada, Natal, Australia, India, Bermuda, etc., as provinces of one continuous territory and their mixed peoples obliged to be under the same administration. It is easy to see that such an administration would be much more difficult to carry on than the method of separate administrations which is used by Great Britain. This was the very reason why the Russian imperial administration had such a difficult task.

Of course, when we compare the Russian Empire with the United States rather than with the British

Empire, we find a closer similarity between the two
countries, since they have similar geographical features
and each country is practically a continent itself. But
the area of the Russian Empire was more than twice
that of the United States. Also, although the population of the United States does not belong to one racial
stock, there is a common bond of language, and from a
cultural and economic point of view there is much
more uniformity among the people of the United States
than is the case among the nationalities of Russia.

The total population of the Russian Empire was
about 175 millions in 1914. Of this figure, about 120
millions were of the Russian race, and this group was
divided into three branches: the Russians proper or
the Great Russians, comprising about 66 per cent of
the total Russian racial stock; the Ukrainians, or
Little Russians, about 27 per cent; and the White
Russians, about 7 per cent. The other groups were
Poles, Turks, Mongols, Finns, and Jews. Some of
the national minorities, as for instance the Poles, developed brilliant civilizations of their own; there were
others who led the primitive life of hunters and nomads.
These national minority groups (particularly the Poles,
the Ukrainians and the Lithuanians) were subject to
various restrictions on their cultural life. They were
obliged to use the Russian language in the courts and
in the public schools. The Jews were subject to special police supervision and were allowed to live only
in the south-western provinces of Russia, within the
so-called "pale of settlement," and only college grad-
uates and rich merchants were granted permits to leave
the "pale."

The majority of the population, that is to say, about

84 per cent, lived in the country and only about 16 per cent in the cities. As regards the social strata of the Russian population, there were, for every thousand of the population, 813 peasants, 128 merchants and townsmen, 26 Cossacks, 17 nobles, 6 clergymen, and 10 belonging to other smaller groups. The Russian nobility had discordant historical origins. In addition to the medieval aristocratic families there were others to whom nobility had been granted by the Imperial power in the eighteenth and nineteenth centuries; then, too, nobility, according to the Russian law, was acquired automatically by membership in 'the higher ranks of both the military and the civil service. Thus nobility was not a closed cast and was constantly being increased by new membership. Only part of the noblemen owned landed estates and resided in the country; the others lived in the cities and led the life of civil servants or intellectuals.

The landowning nobility was an organized body in each province and county, but the landless nobility had practically no special privileges when compared with the middle class of the cities.

The merchants and townsmen differed very little in their social status from their fellows in other European countries. Although the peasants received personal freedom and land in 1861, their legal status differed from that of other citizens until 1906. Each individual peasant was subject to certain restrictions by the village community; he had to ask special leave of absence from the communal authorities in order to move to the city and he used the land as a part of the communal estate and not as his own property. Not until 1906 was the unlimited power of the village commune destroyed by law and each peasant granted the right to demand that the commune apportion his own plot of land to him from the communal holdings.

THE POLITICAL STRUCTURE OF RUSSIA BEFORE THE WAR

Before the Revolution of 1905, Russia was ruled by an autocratic emperor, with the help of bureaucratic agencies. The leading positions in the administration were for the most part held by the members of the landed nobility. There was no central national representative body, but there were provincial and county assemblies, known as Zemstvos, whose authority was confined to the administration of education, public health and other local cultural needs. There were municipal organizations of the same kind in the cities. The provincial governors were appointed by the emperor and had the power of veto over the decisions of the Zemstvos and the municipal organizations.

The bureaucratic régime was less severe than might be expected, because of the fact that since 1864 Russia had had an excellent judicial organization with a well-balanced system of courts discriminating between civil and criminal cases, and the use of a jury in criminal trials. However, there were serious defects in the judicial organization. In the first place, in the villages it applied only to major crimes. In minor cases the peasants were not subject to the general courts but to special officers appointed by the government from the nobility, known as *Zemsky nachalnik*, or Land Captains. These Land Captains had administrative as well as judicial authority over the peasants. Another defect in the Russian courts was the fact that in cases of political crime the secret police had authority to act independently of the court. People under suspicion of participation in political crimes could be arrested, imprisoned, and exiled to Siberia by a simple police order without a court warrant.

The political structure of Russia underwent far-reaching changes in 1905. All over Russia there were strikes, peasant arrests, mutinies in the army, mass meetings, street demonstrations and political banquets. On October 30 (October 17 according to the Julian Calendar [2]), 1905, an imperial manifesto granting a constitution was issued. A parliament of two chambers was organized. The upper chamber was known as the Imperial Council or Council of State. Half of the members of this council were appointed by the emperor, the other half were elected by the Zemstvos and municipal bodies, Chambers of Commerce, provincial nobility, etc. The lower chamber, the Imperial Duma or State Duma, was elected entirely by the nation. The first electoral law was promulgated

[2] The Julian Calendar, or the one introduced by Julius Cæsar, was in general use in Europe from the time of the Roman Empire until it was abolished by Pope Gregory XIII in 1582 and replaced by a modified system of his own. This Gregorian Calendar was adopted immediately by Roman Catholic countries; England accepted it in 1752 but it was not adopted in Russia until 1918. The change of the Calendar had been considered in Russia before the war but it would not have been an easy undertaking then since it would have interfered with the established Church ritual. In the twentieth century the difference between the Julian and the Gregorian Calendar amounted to 13 days. Russian reckoning was therefore thirteen days behind that of the western world. Unless otherwise stated, the dates in this book are indicated according to the Gregorian Calendar.

at the end of 1905 and provided for almost universal, but not equal suffrage. Every new law was to be approved by the Duma and the budget was also subject to its approval. However, the emperor retained some very important prerogatives. The army and navy were under his exclusive control, as were also matters relating to foreign affairs; the cabinet was to be appointed by the emperor and was responsible to him rather than to parliament.

This situation resulted in an acute political conflict between the cabinet and the Duma in 1906-1907. In 1907 the electoral system was changed by an Imperial ukase. Universal franchise remained, but the number of electors representing the peasants and labor population was seriously diminished, while the representation of the wealthier classes—the landowners and the industrialists—was reënforced.

The Duma, elected according to the new franchise in the autumn of 1907, was willing to come to a working agreement with the prime minister, Stolypin. This agreement was in operation for all practical purposes up to the World War, and the years 1907 to 1914 were therefore a period of peaceful legislation. Reforms were carried out in various phases of Russian life, the most important of which concerned the education and legal status of the peasants. Just before the World War the Duma passed a law by which the Land Captains were deprived of their judicial authority over the peasants. Justices of the peace were to be appointed instead, who were to act in connection with the general courts. Many of the reforms of the Duma were, however, curtailed by the Imperial Council. As this latter body depended partly on the emperor's will, there was constant danger of a new conflict between the emperor and the Duma; such a conflict did actually occur during the World War.

POLITICAL PARTIES

There were no authorized political parties in Russia before 1905. Up to that time the organizations which were spoken of as political parties were in reality no more than small secret groups of political plotters. The police department was constantly watching the activity of these groups in order to discover and arrest their leaders. Moderate liberal organizations, moreover, were looked upon as no less dangerous to the autocratic régime than the socialist organizations. The leading underground liberal organization before 1905 was the so-called "Union of Liberation," which was formed in 1902. Liberal landowners, college professors, and lawyers were the leaders in this organization.

There were two socialist parties: the Social Democrats and the Social Revolutionaries. The former adhered to the teachings of Karl Marx and carried on revolutionary propaganda among the factory workers. In 1903 they split into two smaller groups, the Bolsheviks (or majority group) and the Mensheviks (or minority group). The Bolsheviks were active and implacable revolutionists. Their leader was Vladimir Ulianov, known subsequently under his revolutionary pseudonym of Lenin. The Mensheviks were more inclined to compromise with the liberals. The most prominent person among them was the older Russian Social Democrat, George Plekhanov. The Social Revolutionaries were more interested in propaganda among the peasants than among factory workers and their views may be characterized as a kind of agrarian socialism. As for their tactics, they preached revolutionary terror against individual agents of the Imperial Government and they were responsible for many political murders in Russia in the beginning of the twentieth century.

With the formation of the Duma, more normal political conditions resulted and the political parties entered a new period. There were numerous political factions in the Duma. The extreme Monarchists whose slogan was "Back to Autocracy" constituted the so-called "right wing." [3] The center of the Duma was formed by the conservatives and moderate liberals who were in the majority and controlled the Duma. They represented the landowners and the bourgeoisie, and they formed the so-called "Union of October 17," which was the date of the constitutional manifesto of 1905, according to the Julian Calendar; hence they were known as Octobrists. On the whole, they supported the existing political régime as well as the electoral system. They were ready to defend the Duma's prerogatives in case of a conflict with the Imperial power, but would not take the initiative in such action. Prominent among them were the President of the Duma during the war period, Rodzianko, and the Moscow industrialist, Guchkov, who was the Minister of War in the first Revolutionary Cabinet.

The left center of the Duma was formed by the

[3] Russian political parlance of the period used the forms right wing, center, left center, and left wing in connection with the Duma. The advocates of autocracy were also spoken of as the extreme right and the socialists were known as the extreme left.

Constitutional Democrats, or Kadets, who may be roughly compared to the French radicals. The Kadets staunchly opposed the Imperial power. Their aspiration was to create a true parliamentary régime in Russia on the French or the British pattern. They advocated a democratic electoral system and a division of large estates among the peasants on the basis of remuneration of the former owners from the State Treasury. They were backed by the intelligentsia and the middle class in general. Their leader was Professor Miliukov, later Minister of Foreign Affairs in the first Revolutionary Cabinet.

In the left wing were first the Laborites, who were the parliamentary faction representing the Social-Revolutionaries, and second, the Social Democrats, both Bolsheviks and Mensheviks being represented by a few deputies. Because of the deficiencies in the electoral system, the left wing was very weak and the number of its adherents was not proportionate to the actual influence of socialist groups in the country. Kerensky, the future head of the Provisional Government, was a prominent member of the Laborite group in the Duma; but neither Lenin nor Plekhanov were members of the Duma as neither of them lived in Russia before the war.

INDUSTRY AND LABOR

Although even after the adoption of the constitution the political structure of Russia was backward, her economic life had already developed along modern lines. This was especially true of her industries. A veritable Industrial Revolution began in Russia late in the eighteen-eighties; the last decade of the nine-teenth century saw the completion of its first stage.

The minister of finance, Sergius Witte, made every effort to promote and increase Russian industry and was especially interested in attracting foreign capital into the country. French and Belgian money was in-vested in the metallurgical plants in Southern Russia; British interests were connected chiefly with the min-ing and petroleum industries. German capital also had a part in these developments. Foreign investments in Russian industries before the World War amounted to 1,343,461,000 rubles, or one third of the whole capital invested. (One ruble is equal to 51¢.) The French and Belgian investments, if considered together, were valued at 450 million rubles, the German at 378 million rubles, and the British at 226 million rubles. There were, of course, in addition to the foreign enterprises, a number of purely Russian plants, especially in the textile industry of Central Russia. The large metal-lurgical plants under Russian management were chiefly to supply the needs of the army and navy and of the railroads.

During these years, the percentage of increase in output of Russian industry was far greater than that of other capitalist countries. In 1900 the smelting production of pig iron in the United States increased 76 per cent as compared to the output of 1890, while the percentage of increase for Russia during the same period was 220 per cent. However, the volume of production in Russia, even in 1900, was five times smaller than in the United States.

There was a period of stagnation during the first years of the twentieth century. A new stage of rapid increase occurred in the years between 1907 and the outbreak of the World War and in certain branches of industry the development continued even during the war until the Revolution of 1917. The production of pig iron in Russia in 1909 amounted to 2.8 million metric tons and in 1913 to 4.6 million metric tons. The increase for five years was 61 per cent. With regard to the output of coal, the increase in five years was 41 per cent. For the same period in the United States the increase was only 24 per cent, and in Great Britain only 7 per cent. Of course, in spite of rapid progress, the volume of industrial production in Russia was still behind that of other capitalistic countries and was not adequate to meet its needs. This shortage was felt particularly during the World War.

A steady increase was also noticeable in the network of railroads. In 1893 there were about 19,000 miles of railroads in Russia, while by 1911 there were 44,000. The number of factory and railroad workers increased correspondingly with the development of industry and railroads. There were 768,759 factory workers in Russia in 1887. By 1912 this number had increased to 2,320,000.

Conditions were bad among the factory workers before the Revolution of 1905, for the wages were low and the working day long, a limit of 11½ hours having been fixed by the law of 1897. Workers were neither allowed to form trade unions nor to strike, and, being deprived of legal means of struggle, they were naturally inclined to listen to revolutionary propaganda. A law was passed, however, in 1906, permitting the formation of trade unions and, in spite of the fact that they were still subject to police supervision, unions began to spread rapidly over the country. The workers were also given the right to take part in the elections of the members of the Duma, but were to vote in primaries in a separate group and had far fewer electors than necessary to give them the representation they deserved according to their numerical importance.

An important law, passed by the Duma in 1912, provided for accident insurance. With the help of the trade unions the workers were able to bring about some improvements in their hard lot. The working day was gradually shortened, the average by 1912 being 10 hours. Wages were also slightly increased, the average wage being 313 rubles a year in 1912. However, these measures were insufficient to satisfy the demands of the majority of the factory workers, and since they were discontented they were quite ready to support Lenin in 1917.

BANKING, FINANCE, AND COMMERCE

The Industrial Revolution in Russia was intimately connected with the growth of banking and finance. The banking and financial system centered about the State Bank which, under the administration of Witte, became a mighty financial weapon in the hands of the Government. According to its charter, the State Bank was directly subordinate to the Ministry of Finance. The policy of the managers of the State Bank was to promote industrial development either directly or through private banks, and in 1913 the sum given by the State Bank in discount and advance operations to private banks amounted to 4,500,000,000 rubles. Another policy of the State Bank was to place certain industries, such as those of coal, iron, sugar, and oil under its control. The bank materially assisted the grain trade of the country by constructing grain elevators at the main railroad stations in South Russia. Several of the private banks were controlled by foreign interests—French, British, or German. Before the war the total capital, deposits, and current accounts in the private banks, amounted to 4,000,000,000 rubles.

A peculiar feature of the Russian financial system before the war was the rapid growth of Government savings banks and petty credit institutions. These banks flourished in the cities and in the country, and had deposits amounting to more than 2,000,000,000 rubles. An important measure in regard to currency was the introduction of the gold standard in 1897. The Russian financial system was able to maintain itself intact on this basis up to the time of the outbreak of the World War, in spite of the Russo-Japanese War and the internal troubles of 1905. The maintenance of the gold basis was connected with the tariff policy and required a favorable balance of trade. For this reason, imports were curtailed by high customs duties and exports were encouraged. The success of this policy is demonstrated by the fact that in 1913 the exports amounted to 1,520,000,000 rubles and the imports to only 1,374,000,000 rubles. Foreign loans were an important part of the Russian State budget; the majority were floated in France. Russian indebtedness to France on the eve of the World War amounted to 3,869,000,000 rubles.

The active rôle of the Government in promoting both financial and industrial progress as well as in attracting foreign capital must be emphasized. The Government did interfere more with the economic life of the country than was the case in Western Europe and in America.

AGRICULTURE

For a long time Russian agricultural development lagged behind that of industry and finance. There was a considerable depression in agriculture during the first period of industrialization, and only during the second period of industrial activity, just before the World War, did extensive changes begin. The growth of agriculture in that period can be shown by the fact that wheat exports, which amounted to 1.9 million metric tons in 1900, increased to 6.2 million ten years later. A similar increase was to be noted in dairy products. The situation may be summed up by the statement that the value of the total agricultural production of Russia in 1913, within the boundaries of the future Soviet Union, amounted to more than 12,000,-000,000 rubles as compared with 6,000,000,000 rubles for industrial production.

This rapid increase in agricultural production was due, in large part, to an improvement in methods on both the large and small farms. The nobles owned most of the large farms. Since the emancipation act of 1861, their traditional methods of farming had been to rent small plots of land to the neighboring peasants. This had resulted in a predominance of backward methods on both the large and small farms. During the next decades, the noblemen, who because of their extravagant ways of living were always in need of money, were obliged to sell part of their land to the peasants and the merchants.

By the end of the eighteen-seventies the nobles owned only about 200,000,000 acres, while 353,000,000 acres belonged to the peasant communes, and by 1905 the peasant holdings had increased to 400,000,000 acres, and the nobles had only 135,000,000. From 1906 to 1914 the peasants acquired 27,000,000 acres more. Although, on the whole, the amount of land owned by the noblemen decreased, those noblemen who retained their land began to attempt to increase the productivity of their farms and the incomes derived from them. Thus before the World War, many of the owners of large farms had dropped the old methods of management entirely and had introduced new machinery. In this way they were converting their farms into purely capitalistic plants, or "grain factories." Similar changes took place in peasant agriculture. In 1906 the individual peasant was granted the right to quit the community and to claim his former share in communal land as his own property.

As individual farmers the peasants were more interested in introducing improved methods on their farms than they had been as members of the village communities, and they were helped in their efforts by the agencies of the Ministry of Agriculture, and by the Zemstvos, the coöperatives, and the petty credit institutions. Year after year the peasants bought more machinery in order to improve their farming methods. In 1908 they purchased 54,000,000 rubles worth of agricultural machinery. In 1912 the amount had increased to 131,000,000 rubles. Of course, most of the peasant fields were still poorly cultivated, but there was decided progress and, what is even more important, this progress was greater every year.

A rapid expansion of the activities of the coöperative societies had a great deal to do with the improvement in the material and mental life of the peasants.[4] Since they were becoming accustomed to having an active part in the economic life of the nation they began to realize what their strength would be if they should combine their efforts. The coöperative societies also helped the peasants to sell their products and to buy manufactured goods without resorting to a middleman. They were especially active in dairy farming and poultry-raising. By 1915 there were more than 30,000 coöperative societies with 12,000,000 members, mostly peasants. The strongest peasant coöperative societies were in Siberia.

EDUCATION AND CULTURAL LIFE

Public opinion has usually credited the Imperial Government of Russia with little desire to promote

[4] By "coöperatives" is meant, in Russian parlance, societies established on the principle of a joint-stock association, each member of which owns only one or a few shares, the shares being very small. Each member has only one vote in the meeting of shareholders.

The petty credit and small loan coöperative associations, which loaned money to their members, were very popular in Russia before the war. There was also a great number of coöperatives organized for the purchase and distribution of commodities for consumption by their members; and, in addition, there were the so-called agricultural coöperatives organized for selling food products from the members' farms. Such coöperatives usually helped the individual members to improve their methods of cultivation as well as to buy new machinery; such, for example, was the case in the production of butter among the peasant farmers in Siberia. In 1908 the first All-Russian congress of coöperatives was held in Moscow; another such congress met in Kiev in 1913.

popular education. It is true that until the Revolution
of 1905 the Imperial Treasury appropriated amazingly small sums for education. But the educational
work of the Zemstvos in that period should not be
overlooked. In the Duma period, the situation changed
entirely. In 1908 the Duma accepted a plan for universal education. At that time the Ministry of Education appropriated a special fund for the construction
of new school buildings throughout the country. In
1908 there were fewer than 100,000 primary schools
in Russia. In the next six years this number was increased by 49,458. In 1914 there were 7,478,000
pupils which was about two-thirds of the total number
of children of school age in the country. This plan
was to have been completed by 1922. This expansion
of educational work was due both to the agencies of
the central government and to the efforts of the local
Zemstvos.

Secondary education also expanded rapidly before
the World War, and there were more than 800,000
students in the various types of high schools. This
expansion was made possible not only by the efforts of
the administration, but also by the donations of private
individuals. As regards Russian universities and technical schools, both the scientific research and the teaching in these institutions before the war were on a level
with the best European and American institutions.

Among various classes of the Russian people there
was an actual thirst for education during the period
before the Revolution. This was especially true among
the factory workers, and, although in a lesser degree,
among the peasants. Boys and girls of the poorest
classes were willing to lead lives of privation in order

to save money for an education. Because of this situation, tuition in government high schools and universities was usually very low, and there were many available scholarships.

The arts, the theater and literature also flourished during this period, and there was a great increase in the number of museums and libraries. There was also an increase in the circulation of newspapers and books. In 1913 there were several hundred newspapers in Russia with a combined daily circulation of 2,728,000. As for books, 34 thousand titles were published in 1913, about 133 million copies in all.

In considering the cultural life of Russia as a whole, it is necessary to note a sharp difference in level between the élite and the masses of the people. Of course, as we have just seen, the rapid spread of new educational facilities which had begun was intended to make the educational levels more equal; but the activity was started too late and could not have attained success by 1917 when the Revolution broke out.

CHURCH AND RELIGION

There were six great religious denominations in the Russian Empire: Eastern, or Greek, Orthodox; Roman Catholics; Protestants; Moslems; Buddhists; and Jews. In addition there were non-conformists (sectarians) who had separated from the Eastern Orthodox Church. The majority of the Russian people belonged either to the Eastern Orthodox Church or to the non-conformists. The Eastern Orthodox Church played as important a part in Russian history as did the Roman Catholic in the history of Western Europe. There was a long period in which this church was the leading force in education and in the whole spiritual life of the people.   During the eighteenth and nineteenth centuries the social and the cultural activities of the church were curtailed by the Imperial Government; an agent of the emperor, the procurator of the Holy Synod, was placed in control of church administration.   At the same time, the Imperial Government put the Eastern Orthodox Church in a privileged position among other denominations, and the non-conformists who left the established church were more or less persecuted until 1905.   The result was a rapid decrease in the moral authority of the Eastern Orthodox Church, and there were no noticeable signs of revival until after 1905.

Among the non-conformists the Old Ritualists, who had separated from the official church in the seventeenth century, considered themselves more Orthodox than the official church.   They were, in many respects, more conservative than the members of the official church.   Other non-conformists, who separated from the official church in the eighteenth and nineteenth centuries, had attempted to simplify the church ritual and the dogma; some of them joined the Baptist Church.   In addition there were anarchistic sects such as the Dukhobors, most of whom migrated to Canada late in the nineteenth century.   There were also a few mystical sects such as the *Khlysty* (Flagellants), who had a strong influence over Rasputin.

THE FOREIGN POLICY OF IMPERIAL RUSSIA

It has been said that Russia made, in spite of many setbacks, a great deal of progress after the Revolution of 1905. There is no doubt but that she had an excellent opportunity to avoid another revolution; but to do this, there was one indispensable condition, namely, that the Imperial Government should keep out of international complications. Such clever statesmen as Witte or Stolypin understood this perfectly. It was a serious misfortune for Russia that, at the time of the European crisis in 1914, Witte was out of power and Stolypin was dead, murdered three years before by a revolutionary agent. The fact must also be considered that Russia's foreign policy was greatly dependent upon the personality of the emperor.

Alexander III (1881-1894) was a pacifist and during his reign the country was at peace. His son Nicholas II, however, wavered between pacifism and a spirit of imperialist adventure. Although he took the initiative in summoning international peace conferences at the Hague in 1899 and 1907, he was at the same time inaugurating an adventurous policy in the Far East which resulted in the war with Japan in 1904. Since the Duma had no jurisdiction over foreign affairs, the emperor was legally in control of such policies. The Duma was only able to deal with such matters at the time when the budget was voted and the expenditures of the Ministry of Foreign Affairs were under discussion. Practically, however, the Duma had assumed more authority in the problems of foreign policy than it had originally been expected to exercise and Izvolsky and Sazonov, the two men who controlled Russia's foreign affairs in the years between the opening of the Duma and the outbreak of the war, were both inclined to act in accordance with the wishes of the majority in the Duma.

In the meantime, great changes were taking place in the general trend of Russian foreign affairs. During most of the nineteenth century until 1890, friendship with Germany (originally with Prussia) was the fundamental principle upon which Russian foreign policy was based. But during the eighteen-nineties there was a *rapprochement* with France, and the Dual Alliance between the two powers (Russia and France) was concluded. In 1904, France entered into an Entente with Great Britain, and Russia followed in 1907. From 1907 on, the Triple Entente of Great Britain, Russia, and France towered before the world as a rival of the Triple Alliance which consisted of Germany, Austria, and Italy. The Octobrists and the Kadets who were in control of the Duma at that time were the parties supporting the Entente, for the Russian liberals were eager to coöperate with the liberal and democratic countries against monarchist Germany. On the other hand, the very existence of the Duma made it more easy for public opinion in France and Great Britain to coöperate with Russia.

The international rivalry between the Triple Alliance and the Triple Entente was reënforced by the rivalries between single members of the two combinations. There was the naval competition between Great Britain and Germany; there was the idea of *revanche* on the part of France; there was the clash of interests between Russia and Austria in the Balkans. Russia, as a Slavonic Power, supported the Jugoslav nationalistic movement which was directed against Austria-Hungary, partly because the latter power had annexed in 1908 two former Turkish provinces populated by Jugoslavs,[5] and partly because Russian political and economic interests in the Near East clashed with those of Austria-Hungary. The leaders in industry and agriculture were looking for an opportunity to gain control of the straits connecting the Black Sea with the Ægean, in order to secure a safe outlet for grain, textiles, petroleum and coal. The straits belonged to Turkey. Russia's influence there and in the Balkans was endangered by the German *Drang nach Osten* [6] and by the expansion of Austria-Hungary in the Balkans.

Furthermore, international financial interests were interwoven with diplomatic problems. Russian industry was a battlefield for the Franco-British and the German interests and in this competition the Franco-British group proved to be the stronger. In addition Russia was financially dependent upon French loans. Therefore Russia was both politically and economically involved in international complications. Under such circumstances it is quite easy to understand that Russia, from several points of view, was not disposed to allow Austria-Hungary to absorb the Jugoslav kingdom in the Balkans. Austria's attack on Serbia consequently led to Russian mobilization and this was followed on August 1, 1914, by the German declaration of war upon Russia.

[5] Bosnia and Herzegovina.

[6] German history, since the days of Charlemagne in the early ninth century, has seemed to many observers a long, gigantic, and continuous drive toward the east (*Drang nach Osten*) at the expense of the Slavs.

RUSSIA IN THE WORLD WAR

The continental character of the Russian Empire and the severe blow to the Russian naval strength administered by the Japanese in 1904-1905, were responsible for the fact that Russia had to rely more on its army than on its navy during the World War.

As for the Russian naval operations, two fields were open: one on the Baltic Sea and one on the Black Sea. Only a few ships had been built since the Japanese War and a few more were under construction when the war began. This small fleet had to oppose the Turks on the Black Sea, and the Germans on the Baltic. The Turkish fleet was even weaker than the Russian, but, at the beginning of the war, two German cruisers in the Mediterranean eluded the French and British fleets and joined the Turkish navy. This paralyzed Russian naval operations in the Black Sea. The Russian fleet in the Baltic conducted some defensive operations against the stronger German navy, but, on the whole, the Russian navy had a passive part in the war and the land operations were of much greater importance.

Russia had to conduct military operations on two fronts: the European, along the western frontier of the Russian Empire, and the Asiatic, along the Turkish frontier in Trans-Caucasia. At the beginning of the war, the Germans took the initiative on land. They attacked France with practically their whole force and left only a feeble shield against Russia. But Austria, on the other hand, threw her main forces against Russia. Thus the primary task of the Russian army was to oppose the Austrians. But, yielding to the demands of the Allies, she attacked East Prussia at the same time in order to force the Germans to transfer some of their troops from the Western to the Eastern front. The result was the failure of the German attack in France; but, at the same time, Germany crushed the two Russian armies which had entered East Prussia. The Germans then entered Russian Poland, but were stopped by the Russians before Warsaw. At the same time the Russians defeated the Austrian armies and occupied the Austrian province of Galicia as far as the Carpathian mountains. These were the results of the autumn campaign of 1914.

In the spring of 1915 the Germans transferred more of their troops from the Western front and began a terrific attack in the East. At that time the Russian armies were in a desperate situation for they did not have enough guns, shells, and rifles. The Russian Imperial Government, like the other governments, had not expected the war to last so long and, consequently, did not have a large enough supply of munitions on hand. Russian industry, in spite of its progress before the war, was still less developed than that of the other capitalistic countries and it was harder for Russia to manufacture additional supplies. The result was a dearth of arms and munitions and the catastrophic retreat of the Russian armies during the entire summer of 1915. The Germans occupied Russian Poland, Lithuania, and some of the White Russian and Ukrainian provinces. Nevertheless, the retreat stopped in the autumn of 1915, and from then on there was a gradual increase in the amount of supplies because of the mobilization of the Russian industries and the shipments of munitions into Russia from Japan and the United States.

In the summer of 1916 the Russian army was able to resume the offensive with partial success. It was undertaken to help the Italians who were in a critical situation. Its main purpose was achieved and Austrian pressure on the Italian front was lessened. Another result was the entrance of Rumania into the war on the side of the Allies. This, however, proved to be a disadvantage to Russia. The Rumanian army was poorly organized and insufficiently equipped. The Germans easily forced it to retreat and as a result Russia had to send troops and supplies to the relief of Rumania. Russia also had to engage in military operations on the Caucasian front against the Turkish armies. In 1916 the Russians had considerable success in Asia Minor and in the direction of Mesopotamia.

A clear conception of Russia's part in the war may be gained by noting the fact that in January, 1917, there were 187 enemy divisions on the Russian fronts and only 132 enemy divisions on the Western front. The Russian command was preparing a general attack for the next spring; but these plans were interrupted by the outbreak of the Russian Revolution.

INFLUENCE OF THE WAR UPON NATIONAL ECONOMY

From the beginning of the war until the outbreak of the Revolution the Russian army suffered severe defeats; but there were also successes and, on the whole, the military position of Russia was more favorable in the spring of 1917 than it had been in the summer of 1915. It was not in the realm of military operations, however, but in other fields that Russia's chief danger resided. Her political organization and her economic system were inadequate to cope for long with the complicated problems that arose from the war. The war affected every phase of her economic life: finance, industry, commerce, agriculture. In the field of finance, the revenues of the Empire decreased and expenditures rapidly increased. Before the war the yearly expenditure of the Russian Empire had been 3.4 billion rubles; for the second half of 1914 the additional war expenditure was 2.5 billion rubles. In 1915 the figure was 8.8 billion and in 1916, 14.5 billion. Although most of these sums were met with the help of Allied loans, the Treasury had to make additional issues of paper money. With the resulting inflation the parity of the ruble, which compared with the pound sterling ($4.86) 9.4 before the war, was 15.5 in 1916.

This great war expenditure was due to the huge number of troops called to the colors. Partly at the request of the Allies, the Russian Government called about 15 million men into the army. This was more men than were actually required and a greater number than could be adequately equipped for duty at the front. This summoning of such a large number of men had grave consequences on the national economic situation. The Government had to feed this huge army and to pay allowances to the families of most of them as well. In addition the nation lost the services of millions of agricultural laborers and, as the war progressed, a serious food problem began to loom on the horizon. Large amounts of food were required for the army daily and, since the fare of a soldier was better than that of the average peasant, more food was needed in war time than in peace time.

Of course, the decrease in exports meant a saving in food products; but, on the other hand, there were new difficulties in transporting the food supplies from South Russia to the North. The railroads were not equipped to meet the additional burdens of war. They were over-crowded with supplies for the army and were unable to meet the needs of the industrial areas of Northern and Central Russia, and of the big cities. Food rationing in the cities and the increased cost of living caused a slackening of the morale of the factory workers. As a result there were many strikes. When the workers demanded higher wages they usually got them, but this caused a rise in the prices of factory products and was responsible for a corresponding rise in the cost of living.

THE POLITICAL CONFLICT

The economic crisis caused by the war was the more serious because it was combined with a political crisis which began to appear in the second year of the war. At first the Russian people supported their Government almost unanimously. They responded willingly to the call to colors and mobilization was carried on in an orderly fashion. In order to facilitate mobilization an Imperial ukase prohibited the sale of liquors. Factory workers in Petrograd ended a strike which they had begun in July, 1914. When the Duma met soon after the beginning of the war, all of the political groups except the Bolsheviks made declarations in support of the war. Lenin, the Bolshevik leader, who was abroad at that time, took a definite stand of opposition. In November, 1914, five Bolshevik deputies in the Duma formally approved his defeatist position. They were promptly arrested, tried and deported to Siberia and no other opposition was noticeable.

But the political truce was short-lived. In the autumn of 1915 relations between the Cabinet and the Duma became tense. The Russian political leaders were worried about the unpreparedness of the Government and its apparent inability to meet the situation which was reflected in the retreat of the Russian army in 1915. At least this was the opinion of the politicians in the Duma. "You must not expect to win the war as long as such fools are in control of the country." In these words one of the leaders of the Kadets expressed his feelings at his party's meeting.

Various national organizations were formed to help the situation. The Zemstvo and Municipal committees took charge of the relief of the sick and wounded soldiers, while the War Industry committees were responsible for the increase in the production of war munitions. These committees were recognized by the Imperial Government and they helped materially to cope with the situation. But the emperor looked with suspicion upon these national committees. They centered around the Duma and the emperor and his advisors from the extreme right wing feared political opposition of that body. The emperor was a man of weak will and was influenced by his energetic, though hysterical wife, the Empress Alexandra, who was the real head of the reactionary movement. She herself was under the hypnotic influence of Rasputin, a Siberian peasant who posed as a prophet. In their turn, the political leaders suspected the emperor, and even more the empress, of secret preparations for a separate peace with Germany. Later investigations in the Imperial Archives proved these suspicions to be unfounded, but they were an important phase of the political psychology of the period.

The conflict between the emperor and the Duma resulted in a deadlock, since neither party was ready to make concessions. The Duma majority demanded that the Cabinet be appointed according to its wishes, but the emperor was not willing to consent to this. Under pressure from the Duma, he was obliged to change his Cabinet ministers constantly, but none met with its approval.

Meanwhile, the political situation became more acute as the Bolsheviks were agitating among the workers, who were very susceptible to influence because of their economic troubles. It was apparent that a way had to be found out of the *impasse*. Groups of political leaders began to discuss plans for drastic action. The result was that Rasputin was murdered on December 30, 1916, by a young aristocrat related to the Imperial family. This, however, did not improve the situation, as it only served to embitter the emperor. Then plans were made for a palace revolution in order to compel the emperor to abdicate. Above all, quick action was necessary; but instead, the situation dragged on, and before the palace *coup d'état* could be carried out, there was a street revolution in Petrograd.[7]

Thus the burden of the war proved to be unbearable

[7] The city of St. Petersburg, founded by Peter the Great in 1703 and made by him the capital of Russia, was renamed Petrograd in August, 1914, immediately after the beginning of the World War. The substitution of the Slavonic form of the city's name for the German was an expression of nationalistic feeling

for Russia. The fact that the political and economic reconstruction of Russia which followed close on the heels of the Revolution of 1905 was well under way in 1914 but in no sense complete, certainly made matters a great deal worse. The forces of the old régime in Russia, capitalizing the emergency in which Russia found herself, were strong enough to check momentarily the liberal and social movement despite its momentum; the result, hardly surprising it would seem, was that the explosion, when it came, was terrific. That explosion, which we call the Russian Revolution of 1917, almost literally "shook the world"; it has certainly altered fundamentally every aspect of Russian life.

connected with the war. In 1924, after the death of Lenin, the Communistic Dictator of Russia, the city was renamed Leningrad, i.e., City of Lenin. Since 1918 Petrograd has no longer been the capital of Russia, the site of the government having been transferred to Moscow in that year.

CHAPTER II

THE MARCH AND THE NOVEMBER
REVOLUTIONS OF 1917

THERE were two stages in the Russian Revolution of 1917. The first was a direct continuation of the struggle between the emperor and the Duma, between Autocracy and Liberalism; the second resulted in the overthrow of the Liberal-democratic system by Bolshevism, which was the aspect of the extreme Socialist aspirations peculiar to Russia. The first began with the election on March 12, 1917 (February 27, Julian Calendar), of the Duma Committee which was to lead the movement. In Russia this is called the "February Revolution," although students in Western Europe refer to it as the "March Revolution." The second stage began with the meeting of the Second All-Russian Congress of Soviets on November 7, 1917. (October 25, Julian Calendar.) Therefore, although this second stage is known in Russia as the "October Revolution," we shall refer to it as the "November Revolution."

THE FORMATION OF THE NEW GOVERNMENT

A general strike of factory workers was declared in Petrograd at the end of February, 1917. This was a signal for huge street demonstrations in the capital. The people were weary of the war and irritated by

37

bread lines, and by the scarcity and high price of food. Although the food difficulties at that time were not as serious then as they became later during the Civil War, for there was no real famine, nevertheless, the people were nervous and were not psychologically ready to face such a situation. Troops from the Petrograd garrison were summoned to quell the movement, but, instead of supporting the Government, they fraternized with the workers. On March 12, most of the troops of the Petrograd garrison had mutinied and officers who tried to control the situation were murdered.

Up to this time the movement lacked a directing center. But on March 12 several regiments set out for the Tauride Palace which was the meeting place of the Duma. The emperor was at the Army Headquarters in Mogilev when he received the first reports of the events in Petrograd. Two ways out of the difficulty were open to him, to yield to the popular movement by appointing a liberal Cabinet agreeable to the majority of the Duma, or to attempt by sheer force to crush the opposition of both the Duma and the workers. The leaders of the Duma and of the army recommended the first method. Members of the Imperial Family, with the exception of the Empress Alexandra, also supported this policy. But during the most critical days Nicholas wavered. By the time he chose the second alternative it was already too late. On March 11, on the eve of the very day when the popular movement began to center about the Duma, he signed a ukase discontinuing that body. At the same time two battalions were dispatched to Petrograd from Headquarters. Neither of these measures could have saved

time on the royal family was under arrest and lived in
their palace under guard.

THE FIRST ASPECT OF THE REVOLUTION

The Revolution swept over Russia with one stroke.
Every one was willing to coöperate and was eager to
recognize the authority of the new Government. Even
the monarchist party made no opposition, since the
Romanovs themselves by official acts had confirmed
the upheaval. The troops and the civil servants took
an oath immediately to support the new régime. Most
of the civil servants remained at their posts; but the
provincial governors were dismissed at once by order
of the new Prime Minister, and their places were taken
by the Zemstvo chairmen. The railroad men accepted
the new order even before the abdication of the emperor. Thus it first seemed that the Revolution would
not stop the functioning of the military machine or of
the civil administration.

In a few days the Allied countries recognized the
Provisional Government. The first to make this move
was the Government of the United States. By that
time the United States had already broken off relations
with Germany and her participation in the war was
practically a certainty. The Russian Revolution, however, strengthened the position of those Americans who
advocated entrance into the war. The downfall of
Russian autocracy made Allied propaganda much
easier; for after March 1917, the German coalition
could be described with some force as the only remain-
ing bulwark of autocracy, and all of the Allied countries as adherents of a democratic system of govern-

ment of some kind. Also, the apparent reason for the
Liberal revolution in Russia had been the incapacity
of the Imperial Government to conduct the war with
sufficient energy. The Liberals had been afraid that
the Imperial Government would conclude a separate
peace with Germany. Thus it is no wonder that the
victory of the Liberals was understood both in the
Allied countries and in America to be a pledge for
greater effectiveness in carrying on the war operations.

THE CONTRADICTIONS OF THE REVOLUTION

It was soon easy to see that what had appeared at
first to be the real face of the Revolution was only a
mask; the inner contradictions of the Revolution were
very quickly revealed. In the first place, there was a
complete lack of understanding between the Liberal
Government and the masses of the people. While the
former advocated a most energetic continuation of the
war, the latter were completely weary of the war in
all its phases.

The Petrograd factory workers and soldiers had
marched to the Duma building on March 12 because
they knew the Duma was willing to overthrow the
Imperial Government. But the Duma opposed the emperor because it wished to carry on the war more
energetically while the Petrograd workers and soldiers
fought the Imperial administration in order to rid
themselves of the burden of war. Thus it was an un-
natural union from the very first. This was emphasized by section 7 of the first program of the Provisional Government which promised the soldiers of

the Petrograd garrison that they would not be sent to the front.[1]

In the second place, it became increasingly clear that there was a conflict between the Provisional Government appointed by the Duma and the Soviet, organized by Socialist leaders, a conflict between Liberalism and Socialism. This conflict was not so much a result of actual political differences as it was of the inveterate suspicions which each side had of the other. Both the Liberals and the Socialists were agreed on the necessity for a democratic system of administration. Nevertheless, the Socialists were haunted by constant fears that the Liberals would later become reactionary and would crush the Socialist movement by force. On the other hand, the Liberals were afraid that the Socialists would not support the continuation of the war. The Socialist position may be partly explained by the Marxian dogma to which they adhered. Marx's pamphlet on the French Revolution of 1848 was almost a gospel for Russian Socialists of 1917 and they expected the Russian Revolution to follow its course. They were quite sure that, according to the French pattern, the Russian Liberals would prepare a counter-revolution and would open the way for a dictatorship of the Napoleonic type. Therefore, they were primarily concerned with the necessity of preventing the formation of a strong central government, for they feared that such a government would become reactionary. It was not until much later, in 1930, after a decade of exile that the first Socialist member of the Provisional Government, Kerensky, admitted that, in

[1] See above, p. 40.

reality, there had been another way open to the leaders of the Russian Revolution in 1917, namely, that of a temporary democratic dictatorship. However, they did not see this possibility in 1917. Whatever their reasons, the fact remains that the Socialists tried to counterbalance the Provisional Government, in the capital and in the provinces, by the creation of the system of Soviets.[2]

(From the very beginning of the Revolution, the Socialist leaders paid special attention to the army. They tried to disorganize the existing military administration in order to shift the control of the army from the Provisional Government to the Soviet.) As early as March 14, the Soviet issued the famous "Order No. 1," which was intended to win over the soldiers. According to this order, all military units were to elect soldiers' committees and also representatives to the Soviets. The soldiers were advised to subordinate themselves to the Soviet "in all their political actions." The orders of the Provisional Government "shall be executed only in such cases as do not conflict with the orders and resolutions of the Soviet." It went on to say that "all kinds of arms, such as rifles, machine guns, armored automobiles, and the like, must be kept at the disposal and under the control of the company and battalion committees, and in no case be turned over to officers, even at their demand." It was plain that the result of such an order could only be slackening of discipline, mistrust by the soldiers of their officers, and the disintegration of the army.

The Provisional Government was incapable of pre-

[2] See below, pp. 52 ff.

venting the publication of this order. Only prompt and harsh measures could have been effective. Instead, the Government let itself be satisfied by evasive semi-apologies from the Soviet. The Government tried to take the initiative and created a special committee on the "rights of soldiers." In the meantime sharp conflicts began between officers and men in the army and the navy. There were many cases of lynching of officers, particularly in the navy.

Thus there were soon local Soviets not only throughout the country, but also in the army detachments. The result was confusion in the civil and the military administration. Although the Soviets succeeded in checking the authority of the agents of the Provisional Government, they did not build up a competent administration of their own. The result was a weakening of both civil and military order.

Bolshevik and anarchistic groups of factory workers and intellectuals in Petrograd and in the provincial cities soon took advantage of the weakness of the administration. In Petrograd the Bolsheviks seized the palace of the dancer Kshesinskaya and used it for their headquarters until July, 1917. The anarchists also seized several buildings in Petrograd and in Moscow, and for several months defied police orders to evacuate them. Robbery and drunkenness spread over the cities. The Soviet was obliged to appeal to the population to prevent "lawlessness, fights, and pogroms." The situation was the more disastrous, since the country was still at war. Besides, the whole fabric of national economy had been torn by the effects of the war. At a time when the country needed a particularly strong and able administration, a weak and failing government emerged from the turmoil.

FOREIGN POLICIES OF THE RUSSIAN REVOLUTION

We cannot speak of one definite line of foreign policy in connection with that followed by the leaders of the Russian Revolution. As a matter of fact, they had not less than three divergent programs. The Liberals advocated an energetic conduct of the war. Their spokesman in this respect was Paul Miliukov, the first Minister of Foreign Affairs of the Provisional Government. The Liberals specifically demanded an energetic and immediate offensive on the German front. On the other hand, an immediate cessation of the war was the secret desire of the masses of the population and of the soldiers, although they did not as yet openly express this wish. Their spokesman, Vladimir Lenin, became the Bolshevik leader immediately upon his return from abroad in the middle of April, 1917.

Between these two extremes there was a third war policy which was advocated by the Socialist leaders who were in control of the Soviet at that time. Their slogan was a defensive war. The chief spokesmen for this program were Kerensky and Tseretelli. For some time this policy was very popular among all those who were ashamed to express openly their wish for an immediate, even though a separate peace with Germany, and many declared themselves to be in favor of this ambiguous slogan of a defensive war. The result was a gradual shifting of the official Cabinet position concerning war aims.

The first step taken by the Minister of Foreign

Affairs, Miliukov, was to notify all the Allied Governments that Russia did not intend to change her foreign
policy and would be faithful to her Allies. "Faithful
to the pact which unites her indissolubly to her glorious
Allies, Russia is resolved, like them, to assure the world,
at all costs, an era of peace among the nations, on the
basis of stable national organization, guaranteeing respect for right and justice. She will fight by their side
to the end against the common enemy without cessation
and without faltering."

The Soviet could not agree with Miliukov's point of
view and ten days later, on March 27, issued its own
appeal "To the proletarians and toilers of all countries." In this appeal, the Soviet made the following
statement: "We announce that the time has come to
start a decisive struggle against the grasping ambitions
of the governments of all countries; the time has come
for the people to take the power of decision on the
question of war and peace into their own hands." At
the same time, an editorial in the *Izvestia,* the official
paper of the Soviet, protested against the chauvinists'
talk of "a victorious end," and advocated the formula
adopted by the international conferences of the Socialists at Zimmerwald and Kiental.[3] This formula
asked for a "peace without annexations or indemnities
on the basis of the self-determination of peoples."

The conflict was aggravated by the next note of
Miliukov on war aims, issued on May 1, in which he
expressed "the aspirations of the entire nation to carry

[3] These conferences took place in 1915 and 1916 in Switzerland.
They were organized by those Socialist leaders who had attempted
to stop the war by pacifist proclamations. The Bolsheviks headed
by Lenin had an important part in the conferences.

the World War to a decisive victory." "It is obvious," added Miliukov, "that the Provisional Government, while safeguarding the rights of our own country, will, in every way, observe the obligations assumed toward our Allies." The publication of this note led to a sharp conflict between the Provisional Government and the Soviet. Huge street demonstrations were held in Petrograd both against and in support of Miliukov. Representatives of the Allies, by attempting to act as mediators, were also involved in these events. The Allies were ready to accept the Soviet point of view concerning the "annexations," in so far as this point applied to Russia herself, that is, in connection with Russian claims to Constantinople and the Straits. The cancellation of these claims by Russia was agreeable to both Great Britain and to France. At the same time, both the British and the French were afraid that the internal conflict in Russia might weaken her resistance to the Germans. For these reasons, the Allies deemed it necessary to oppose Miliukov and to exert pressure on the Russian Government. Through the mediation of the Allies, the Provisional Government decided to compromise with the Soviet. Miliukov and the War Minister, Guchkov, were allowed to resign and the Cabinet was reconstructed.

THE DOMESTIC POLICY OF THE PROVISIONAL GOVERNMENT

The first reconstruction of the Provisional Government resulted in a coalition Cabinet. Several Socialists joined the Cabinet: Kerensky assumed the Ministry of War and the Navy; Chernov, another Social Revolutionary, was given the Ministry of Agriculture; and Tseretelli, a Social Democrat (Menshevik), accepted the Ministry of Post and Telegraph. Now, out of the fifteen members of the Cabinet, six were Socialists. The Bolsheviks, or the extreme left wing of the Socialists, however, were not invited to participate in the Cabinet. They did not support it, and merely waited for the first opportunity to overthrow both the Liberals and the Moderate Socialists; for the former, in their opinion, were reactionary members of the bourgeoisie, and the latter were their agents. As a matter of fact, however, the Socialists were more influential than the Liberals in the new Cabinet. Although Prince Lvov retained his position as Prime Minister, Kerensky became the leading member of the new Cabinet.

Both before and after the reconstruction of the Cabinet, the Provisional Government tried to carry out a number of far-reaching internal reforms, according to the program already mentioned, which was published by the Government immediately after its formation. A new organization of local self-government, both for the Zemstvos and for the municipalities, was introduced. Universal franchise was established and women were to vote on equal terms with men. All details of the electoral system were elaborated by the best available specialists in political science.

The first elections to these new local assemblies were held in the autumn of 1917 and the Social Revolutionaries won the victory at the polls. Both the right and the left wing (the Kadets and the Bolsheviks), however, also received many votes in the local assemblies. This system of local assemblies, of course, was to be crowned by a central national assembly elected by the same universal franchise, with proportional representation of the voting parties. The first national assembly to be elected according to the universal franchise, moreover, was to be endowed with constituent powers for the final organization of the Russian Government. This contemplated first assembly was spoken of as the Constituent Assembly. Accordingly, the Provisional Government organized a special committee to prepare for the summoning of this Assembly. Since lists of voters were to be registered with the boards of the new local government, these elections were bound to take place somewhat later than the formation of the new Zemstvo and municipal bodies. Thus the elections for the Constituent Assembly, first announced for September, 1917, had to be postponed; they were later definitely set for November 25, 1917.

In addition to the problem of central and local national representation, the Provisional Government also had to deal with projects of judiciary organization and popular education. Russia had an excellent judicial system even before the Revolution, and it was only necessary for the Provisional Government to abolish a few limitations upon its independence introduced by Alexander III and Nicholas II, meanwhile extending the power of justices of the peace over the villages. It also made, naturally, many appointments of men of democratic spirit to the various branches of higher judicial administration.

According to the Liberals, the chief weakness of the imperial system of justice was not the organization of the judicial administration proper, but the constant interference of the secret political police. Now not only were the evil practices of the political police eliminated, but this institution was entirely abolished. Moreover, the regular police force was completely reorganized; the former personnel was dismissed and the newly enlisted members were put under the control of the municipal and Zemstvo bodies. The organization of the new police force was, however, not a success because the new corps was entirely inexperienced and unable to cope with the situation which confronted it.

In the matter of education, the Provisional Government decided to push the program of universal education already elaborated by the Imperial Government. The new Government was ready to transfer the whole control of education to the teachers' unions. All-Russian conferences of teachers in secondary and elementary schools were held in order to consider freely the problems of education.

In the matter of the Church, the Provisional Government proclaimed absolute freedom of religious worship. The Eastern Orthodox Church was given freedom of organization independent of interference by the civil administration. The *Sobor*, or general assembly of the deputies of parishes of the Eastern Orthodox Church, led by its bishops, opened in Moscow late in the summer.

It was only natural that the Provisional Government should carry on the program of complete equality for all Russian citizens. All measures against the Jews were abolished. The divisions of society in different orders, such as nobility, merchant guilds and peasants, were abolished; in the future there were to be only equal, free citizens in Russia.

One of the most important problems in the opinion of the revolutionary leaders was that of agrarian reform. It was understood that the privately-owned, larger estates would be divided among the peasants. The Government, however, thought it was its duty to act very cautiously in this matter because of the complexity of the situation. The merchants and richer peasants, as well as the former noblemen, owned farms. There were about three million individually-owned peasant farms which had been separated from the communes by the Stolypin law, and there were about three million more whose owners had already made application for separation. On the other hand, the peasants who were still organized in the communes, above 12,000,000 families in all, seethed with discontent and asked for an immediate redivision among themselves of all available land. The Provisional Government adopted a compromise proposed by Chernov, Minister of Agriculture in the reorganized Cabinet. Special peasant committees were to be formed in each village to act as trustees for the larger estates, pending the final decision of the question by the Constituent Assembly.

THE SOVIETS

While the Cabinet was busy with legislation, the Soviets tried to tighten their grip on Russian politics. They took advantage of the fact that the tempo of the Cabinet's activities was too slow for the nervous mood of the Revolutionary mobs. The Cabinet was elaborating excellent projects for new institutions according to the latest theories of constitutional law, but the committees appointed by the Cabinet worked too carefully at a time when quick action was more necessary than thoroughness. When the Cabinet postponed the convocation of the Constituent Assembly in order to work out the minute details of the electoral system, the Soviets organized a National Assembly of their own. At first the Soviet system was not based on elaborate legal foundations. It was not a true democratic institution but rather an instrument of mob-rule. It had the advantage, however, of being well adapted to the psychology of the revolutionary masses. All factory workers, soldiers and peasants were supposed to participate in the election of a Soviet in every city, regiment, or township. The landowners and the members of the middle class were not admitted to the polls.

It should be noted that only the Socialist parties were recognized by the Soviet leaders. The so-called bourgeois parties, even in cases where they were truly democratic, were excluded from membership. On the other hand, non-party peasants and workers were admitted. The leaders of the Socialist parties were *ex officio* members of the Soviets. Under such conditions, the Soviets were controlled entirely by the Socialist parties. There was no elaborate procedure for elections to the Soviets and no secret ballot. The constituencies voted by raising hands.

In June, 1917, the first All-Russian Congress of Soviets was summoned by the Executive Committee of the local Petrograd Soviet. The strongest group of deputies in this Congress belonged to the Social Revolutionary party; Mensheviks came next in numbers and Bolsheviks were in the minority. The Congress was a bulky body of almost a thousand deputies. There was no serious political work done at this meeting; the leaders harangued the assembly with fiery speeches, and the members followed them passively.

The election of the "All-Russian Central Executive Committee of the Soviets" was the principal result.

This body consisted of about three hundred members and was in future to play the rôle of a Soviet parliament. As a matter of fact, however, the Soviet policy was controlled not by this Committee, but by its *Presidium,* a group of its officials constituting an "inner ring"—a committee within a committee—which consisted of about a score of men, mostly Social Revolutionaries and Mensheviks; very few of these men were factory-workers or peasants, for most of them belonged to that same middle-class which they denounced politically. The Central Executive Committee discussed the policy of the Provisional Government, but the Cabinet ministers were not formally responsible to the Soviet Committee, and only the Socialists among them paid any attention to the resolutions of the Soviets. In many cases, the Central Executive Committee, however, had more real power than the Cabinet, as the former soon succeeded in controlling a considerable military force through the local army Soviets. Deputies of local army Soviets and peasant deputies were constantly calling at the central Soviet office. The Central Executive Committee of the Soviets nominated several committees to consider various problems of administration and finance. These committees had to work simultaneously with the departments of the Provisional Government in order to prepare projects for laws to be considered by the future Constituent Assembly. On the whole, the Soviets were as yet incapable of creating a strong administration of their own, but by their constant interference they certainly did much harm to the Cabinet of the Provisional Government.

THE KERENSKY OFFENSIVE AND THE JULY UPRISING

"Army Order No. 1" contributed a great deal to the disorganization of the Russian army. Soldiers no longer trusted their commanders and officers were afraid of their soldiers. Orders of a commander were no longer executed unless they were confirmed by the army Soviets. The influence of Order No. 1 was the more disastrous as the army was already weary of the war. The new program of a defensive war was understood by the soldiers to be merely a plan to hold their present trenches without any attempts to push the Austro-German army back. Besides, the promise of the Provisional Government not to move the soldiers of the Petrograd garrison to the front produced a demoralizing effect on the soldiers who were already there.

The soldiers' conception of a "defensive war" did not, however, coincide with that of Kerensky, who became Minister of War in the reorganized Cabinet. By the slogan of a defensive war Kerensky meant an attempt to drive the Austro-German army from Russian soil. Since the summer of 1915 the enemy had occupied considerable tracts of Russian territory, and thus a defensive war in the opinion of Kerensky was bound to begin with an attack on the German lines. Kerensky spent several weeks in reviewing troops along the whole front and haranguing them in order to induce them to attack the enemy. This attack actually took place on July 1, 1917, and was successful for a fortnight. The Austrian lines were torn to pieces.

This Russian effort, however, known as "Kerensky's offensive," soon collapsed. The attack had been carried out almost entirely by volunteers, chiefly officers and a few soldiers; after a large number of these volunteers had been either killed or wounded it was impossible to continue. In the meantime, the Germans brought reënforcements from the Western front and began a counter-attack. The Russian army was exhausted; its retreat soon turned into a catastrophe. The Germans could, at this time, have occupied the whole of southern Russia if they had chosen to do so. However, they preferred to wait for the further decomposition of the Russian administration.

At the same time serious unrest had been developing in Petrograd. First, there was a Cabinet crisis when the Liberals disagreed with the Socialists on the question of granting immediate autonomy to the Ukraine. Four Kadet members of the Cabinet resigned. The Bolsheviks tried to use this new conflict to further their own aims. They decided that the moment had come to seize power. They organized huge street demonstrations of armed factory workers; sailors from Russian battleships stationed at Kronstadt, near Petrograd, came to their support. The soldiers of the Petrograd garrison were undecided as to which side they would support. The Bolsheviks almost succeeded in mastering the situation in Petrograd but they were afraid to make a supreme effort and hesitated for some hours. In the meantime, Kerensky recalled a cavalry corps from the front. To make matters worse, the army intelligence service had, at this time, documents at its disposal which, in the opinion of the Cabinet, seemed to prove a financial connection between the Bolsheviks

and the Germans. Some of these documents were given
to the press and produced a great impression, in spite
of refutations by the Bolsheviks. Patriotism was still
strong with the Russian people. After the publication
of these documents of alleged Bolshevik treason, the
soldiers of the Petrograd garrison decided to support
the Provisional Government.

Kerensky was the victor. The Bolshevik leaders
either fled or were arrested. Their headquarters were
raided and they were ejected from the Kshesinskaya
palace. This occurred on July 19, 1917.

THE KORNILOV REBELLION

After this July crisis, the Provisional Government
was reorganized again. The Socialists now received
eight portfolios out of the fifteen in the Cabinet.
Prince Lvov resigned and Kerensky became Prime
Minister, at the same time retaining his post as Minister of War and the Navy. The new Cabinet was
especially anxious to avoid any concessions which
might bring about the much feared bourgeois reaction.
Kerensky tried to hold to a moderate position between
Liberalism and Bolshevism. Although individual leaders of the Bolshevik party were put on trial after the
July uprising, the Cabinet did not outlaw the Bolshevik party as a whole and the latter continued to participate in the Soviet activities.

The position of the Cabinet as the controlling power
over both the country and the army seems to have
begun to improve gradually. There were, however, influential groups both in the country and in the army
which were impatient to form a stronger and a more

active administration. The Bolshevik party was the left wing of the Socialist movement. Following the July crisis a right wing of the Liberal group began to crystallize. Its leaders tried to take advantage of the failure of the Bolshevik uprising to make its own influence paramount. The members of this group now began to consider the Commander-in-Chief, General Kornilov, as their natural leader. He had become famous during the war because of heroic acts and especially by his daring escape from an Austrian prison. He had commanded an army during Kerensky's offensive, had kept his head during the general collapse, and had tried by the use of drastic measures to rebuild the morale of the troops. At the same time, he was known politically as a sincere republican.

Thus it was only natural that he was soon appointed Commander-in-Chief of the Russian armies. He accepted the appointment with the stipulation that he should enjoy complete authority in military questions. This, as a matter of fact, meant the establishment of a military dictatorship at the front. Following his appointment, the Army Headquarters in Mogilev became in reality a center for rising patriotic aspirations. Politicians who were dissatisfied with the Petrograd administration began to visit Mogilev with the hope of founding a new administration there. Although there was not yet a real plot against Kerensky, the psychological background for one had been created.

In appointing Kornilov, Kerensky had promised to support him with the authority of the Government in his attempts to reëstablish military discipline and this had the appearance of a plan for a joint dictatorship of Kerensky and Kornilov. But at this point Kerensky became worried for fear Kornilov would proclaim himself sole dictator. Having been informed of alleged plans of Kornilov, Kerensky dismissed him without hesitation from the position of Commander-in-Chief. Kornilov refused to obey and ordered a cavalry corps to attack Petrograd. Then both Kornilov and Kerensky proclaimed each other traitors.

Kornilov's rebellion soon proved to be a failure. He over-estimated the weight of his name. While he was popular among the Liberals and the Army officers, the Socialists and the men did not trust him, for they suspected that he had made secret plans for the restoration of the monarchy. This was not the case, for he was a staunch republican; but, at the same time, his victory would, of course, have led to some shifting of the political stage towards the right wing. In Kornilov's opinion, the Soviets apparently should have been either disbanded or deprived of their political influence.

There was no actual fighting between the Kornilov and the Kerensky troops; Kerensky won by propaganda. Kornilov's troops began to waver before an engagement could take place, and the commander of his cavalry corps shot himself. Kornilov himself was soon arrested and imprisoned near Mogilev (September 14). It was the Bolsheviks who gained by the conflict between Kornilov and Kerensky. In attempting to rally all available forces against Kornilov, Kerensky was obliged to appeal to the Bolsheviks for help. A Workers' Red Guard was created and this soon became the nucleus of a Bolshevik military force.

THE ECONOMIC CRISIS

As has already been noted, (the war had had a depressing effect upon Russian economic life.) The Revolution did not improve the situation, which became worse every month during the entire summer of 1917. Of course, the general disorganization of the administration was one of the most important reasons for the increasing weakness of the economic situation. As a result of the weakening of labor discipline industrial production was constantly decreasing. The railroads were under the joint administration of the Ministry of Communications and of the Executive Committee of railroad employees and the result was mismanagement and a decrease in car-loadings.

In addition, the factory workers and the railroad men were constantly demanding higher wages. An increase in wages was partly necessary to meet increased living expenses, but higher wages meant a rise in the prices of commodities which would in turn bring a higher cost of living. In the meantime, the treasury had to issue more paper money. This inflation was another cause for the increase in prices. The rate of exchange on Petrograd checks in London, which was 22 rubles per pound sterling in July, by September had risen to 32.

The disorder in industry and finance was paralleled by an agricultural crisis. Agriculture was in a state of confusion. The larger estates suffered from *sabotage* by the hired laborers and the neighboring peasants. In many cases the peasants had seized part of the land and pastures of the large estates and had destroyed the buildings on them and had killed the owners. The small individual farmers also were subject to attack from neighboring peasant communes. On the village communal farms, production did not diminish, but it had never been large enough and now the peasants were unwilling to sell their grain since money was losing its value and commodities were becoming scarce.

The Government tried to meet the situation by establishing a grain monopoly. According to this law, any grain that the peasants wished to dispose of could only be sold to Government agents at fixed prices. The natural results was that the peasants began to hoard their grain. The economic confusion was made more serious because the Government had the difficult task of supplying the army, for although the soldiers stopped fighting, they did not stop eating.

THE BOLSHEVIK ASCENDANCY

The economic crisis was even more dangerous for Kerensky's Government than was the situation created by the political complications. In July Kerensky was victorious against the extreme left and in September against the extreme right, but when he had to cope with the economic collapse, he failed.

He tried to find a way out by calling committees and conferences. The committees discussed the question of disbanding part of the army, of raising the fixed price for grain, and of improving discipline in the factories. Some of these plans had merit, but it was obvious that rapid action was necessary above everything else. Instead, there was a flood of oratory. It was not until the end of October that acting Minister of War, General Verkhovsky, proposed an immediate conclusion of peace as the only action that could save the situation. He did not receive the support of his colleagues and was forced to resign. A fortnight later, the Bolsheviks seized the power.

The ascendancy of the Bolsheviks began after the failure of Kornilov's rebellion. Russia was like a pendulum, swinging to the left in July, to the right in September, and to the left again in November. By October, 1917, the Bolsheviks were in control of the Petrograd Soviet. Trotsky became its chairman. This was a very important event, because the Soviet of the capital was naturally the leader of the local Soviets. There was an All-Russian Central Executive Committee of the Soviets which was still under the control of the Social Revolutionaries and Mensheviks, but this Committee was rapidly becoming unpopular with the masses, since it shared the original sin of the Provisional Government; although it considered, deliberated, and passed resolutions. it did not actually lead the administration.

While this Committee was wasting time in deliberations, the Bolsheviks with great energy organized new groups, or "cells," as they were called, among the Petrograd factory workers and the soldiers of the Northern Russian army. Since they were now the leaders in the Petrograd Soviet, they easily got control of the Petrograd workers' Red Guard as well. These were armed bands of factory workers, formed during the Kornilov rebellion to oppose his troops. The Soviet soon appointed a Military Revolutionary Committee to command the Red Guard.

Lenin was the real head of the Bolshevik movement. He was not in Petrograd at that time and was directing events from Finland where he had gone into hiding after the July uprising. Leading articles written by him were published by the Bolshevik press throughout the country. Following Lenin's plan, the Bolshevik propaganda concerned itself chiefly with Kerensky's incapacity to meet the economic situation. Lenin promised to take the following drastic steps to solve this problem: to conclude an immediate peace, to place industry under the workers' control, and to distribute the land to the peasants. In addition, he proposed a rigid system of food rationing in the cities; the enemies of the Soviets were to be deprived of food-cards and in this way forced to surrender. The banks were to be "nationalized" and all private capital was to be confiscated.

This program appealed to the factory workers and the soldiers. Lenin tried to gain the sympathies of the street mobs by arousing a feeling of envy among all the poor against the more well-to-do, by throwing such slogans to them as "peace to huts, war to the palaces," "loot the looters," and others of the same kind.

THE VICTORY OF THE BOLSHEVIKS

By the end of October, Lenin felt that the time was ripe for an upheaval and began to speed up his activities. He reëntered Russia secretly from Finland and hid in the suburbs of Petrograd. On October 23, he took part in a meeting of the Central Committee of the Bolshevik party and a resolution was passed on the necessity of an armed uprising. On November 4, the Military Revolutionary Committee of the Petrograd Soviet issued instructions to the soldiers of the Petrograd garrison to obey only those official staff orders which had been confirmed by the Committee.

This was open rebellion. In spite of the situation, the Provisional Government could not shake off its lethargy. It was not until November 6 that it ordered the military cadets to guard the Winter Palace, which was the seat of the Government. This had little effect upon the situation, for all other troops of the Petrograd garrison went over to the Bolsheviks and the sailors of the Russian navy joined them. One battleship entered the Neva River in order to be ready to fight in case of need. Late in the evening of November 6, Lenin came in disguise to the headquarters of the Petrograd Soviet to take charge of the movement. During the night the Bolshevik troops occupied all the chief government buildings, the main telegraph office, and the railway stations. The Winter Palace was besieged during the day of November 7, and the Government surrendered that same night. Kerensky, however, had managed to ecape on the morning of the same day and had left Petrograd by automobile.

Meanwhile, the Second All-Russian Congress of Soviets opened its session. Although the Bolsheviks did not have the majority they were the most numerous faction and succeeded in getting control of the whole body because of a split within the Social Revolutionaries, the next largest party. The right wing of the Social Revolutionaries, as well as the Mensheviks, left the Congress, but the left wing of the Social Revolutionaries went over to the side of the Bolsheviks. The Soviet Congress proclaimed itself the supreme power in the country in the place of the Provisional Government.

A new Government was formed, the Cabinet bearing the name of the Council of People's Commissars. Lenin was its chairman; Trotsky was made Commissar for Foreign Affairs; Rykov, Commissar of the Interior; and Stalin, Commissar for Nationalities. At the same time a new Central Executive Committee of the Soviets was elected. The Social Revolutionaries and the Mensheviks had controlled the previous Central Executive Committee. The Bolsheviks controlled the new one; Kamenev, one of their leaders, was elected chairman.

FIRST STEPS OF THE SOVIET GOVERNMENT

The program of the new Soviet Government consisted of three points: peace—for all, land—for the peasants, control over the factories—for the workers, and it immediately turned its attention to the questions of peace and land.

The peace "decree," as a matter of fact, was a proposal of the new Workers' and Peasants' Government "to all warring peoples and their governments that negotiations leading to a just peace begin at once." A statement followed concerning the necessity of peace "without annexations and indemnities." The secret treaties concluded by the former Russian government were annulled "immediately and unconditionally." Finally, the new Government proposed "to all governments and the peoples of all belligerent countries to conclude an armistice of no less than three months at once."

The land decree consisted of two incongruous parts; one, written by Lenin, who was also the author of the peace decree, provided for the confiscation of the large estates; the other, a project elaborated by the Social Revolutionaries, was a program of systematic and rather idealistic "socialization" of land. The first section of this project was as follows: "The right of private ownership of land is abolished forever. Land cannot be sold, bought, leased, mortgaged, or alienated in any manner whatsoever. All lands—state, appanage, cabinet, monastery, church, entail, private, communal, and any other kind—pass to the nation without indemnification and are turned over for the use of those who will till them." The land was to be divided equally among the peasants according to the number of "eaters" in each family and their labor capacity. The aim of this law was to create an ideal peasant commune based on a just distribution of wealth. Lenin, personally, did not sympathize with such a program, since he advocated class war in the villages as well as in the cities. His acceptance of the project of the Social Revolutionaries was a tactical move, by which he won the support of the left wing of the Social Revolutionaries and the sympathies, or at least the non-interference, of those peasants who supported the Social Revolutionary party which was, for the moment, the most popular party in the villages.

There remained the third item of the Bolshevik program: the workers' control over the factories. Consideration of this measure was postponed for a while as it obviously required special attention, involving as it did the introduction of a new economic system. But in order to give some immediate gratification to the workers, Lenin instructed the new Commissar of the Interior, Rykov, to decree the "municipalization" of all private homes and apartments in the cities.

Local Soviets were given the right both to expel the bourgeoisie from their living quarters and to introduce new inhabitants (factory workers) forcibly into their homes. Furniture and other property of the former owners were to be left for the use of the newcomers.

The circulation of these decrees was the first business of the new Soviet Government, for it hoped thereby to win the sympathies of the masses of the people. But before these alleged sympathies could be utilized, the new administration had to undertake another serious task, that of defending its very existence. Kerensky, who escaped from Petrograd on the very day of the Bolshevik Revolution, was summoning troops from the front in order to use them against the Bolsheviks. He succeeded in gathering only a few Cossack detachments. Most of the army was neutral and the officers either mistrusted Kerensky or were indifferent. Besides, the more active of them had either been arrested or dismissed by Kerensky himself after the Kornilov rebellion. As for the soldiers, they were interested in nothing but an opportunity to stop fighting and were not willing to take part in new military activities. Moreover, the Railway Union Committee, attempting to act as mediator between the Bolsheviks and the Socialist groups, stopped the transportation of troops to Kerensky from the front.

Thus, under the circumstances, Kerensky's advance on Petrograd soon proved to be a failure. The Cossacks, who were badly outnumbered, surrendered after an unsuccessful attempt to pierce the Bolshevik lines. Kerensky was obliged to go into hiding to save his life. He managed to escape abroad and disappeared from the political horizon for the whole period of the Civil

War which followed the Bolshevik seizure of power. It was only a decade later that he began again to play a prominent rôle as the head of the democratic group of Russian *emigrés*.

Simultaneously with Kerensky's attempt, there was an uprising against the Bolsheviks in Moscow. A few thousand military cadets and university students made a desperate stand in support of the Provisional Government against those regiments of the Moscow garrison which had turned Red. The majority of the soldiers of the garrison were still neutral. After a week of fighting the Bolshevik troops were victorious.

During both the Kerensky advance and the Moscow uprising, the Soviet Government was obliged to seek an understanding with some of the other Socialist groups. As has been seen, the left wing of the Social Revolutionaries was already backing the Soviet Government. The position of the Railway Union's Committee became of utmost importance to the Soviet Government since it could control the transportation of troops. Lenin started negotiations with the Railway Union on the subject of the formation of a united Socialist Cabinet which was to include representatives of various Socialist groups. It was because of these parleys that the Railway Union had stopped the transportation of the Kerensky troops. Immediately after his victory over both Kerensky and the Moscow uprising, Lenin stopped the parleys with the Railway Union, since its support was no longer indispensable to him. These tactics provoked dissatisfaction within the Bolshevik party itself. Rykov resigned his post of Commissar of the Interior and Kamenev gave up the chairmanship of the Central Executive Committee of the Soviets.

Their posts were immediately filled by other Bolsheviks, and, no further opposition being forthcoming, a political crisis was prevented. Immediately other and greater tasks confronted the Soviet Government.

At first the Soviet Government was in control only in the large cities. At that time the towns and villages were practically under the control of local Soviets, and in November most of these local Soviets had not yet become Bolshevik. It was only gradually that the Central Government succeeded in extending its control over the whole country.

THE DISSOLUTION OF THE ARMY AND THE BEGINNING OF PEACE PARLEYS

A natural result of the Bolshevik *coup d'état* was extreme confusion in the army. After the disappearance of Kerensky, his chief of staff, General Dukhonin, proclaimed himself Commander-in-Chief of the army with headquarters at Mogilev. His fate, however, was determined from the beginning.

Lenin tried to hasten the conclusion of peace with the Germans, for he felt this to be the only means by which matters might be settled in Russia. As the peace decree had had no immediate practical results, Lenin ordered General Dukhonin to start direct parleys with the German army commanders. When Dukhonin hesitated, Lenin dismissed him from his post and appointed the sub-lieutenant, Krylenko, in his place. The latter subsequently became well known as a Chief Soviet State Prosecutor. At the same time Lenin issued an appeal to the soldiers urging them to support the new Government and proclaimed General Dukhonin an obstacle in the way of peace. Soon after the arrival of Krylenko, the new Commander-in-Chief, at headquarters with a squad of sailors, the infuriated soldiers and sailors lynched Dukhonin. The headquarters were disbanded and the brain of the Russian army ceased to exist. Rapid disintegration of the whole army followed. It was a veritable "self-demobilization." Whole detachments left the trenches, sold their munitions and tried to get home either on foot or by railroad; the soldiers filled up the railroad carriages and ejected the civilian passengers wherever there were not enough places for all.

Under such conditions the peace negotiations began. The Soviet delegation asked the Germans to recognize the principle of a "peace without annexations and indemnities" as a starting point for the parleys. The Germans agreed, but with the stipulation that all of the belligerents should join. After this first move the parleys were suspended in order to give the Allies time to act.

THE PARTY STRUGGLE, THE BEGINNING OF TERROR AND THE DISBANDING OF THE CONSTITUENT ASSEMBLY

The victory over Kerensky's weak forces had been comparatively easy for the Soviet Government. It was much more difficult to handle the general political situation. Although the masses of the people did not at first openly resist the Bolshevik power, the Bolshevik party was undoubtedly in the minority. The elections to the Constituent Assembly, held on November 25, 1917, proved this. The election day had been fixed by the Provisional Government before the Bolshevik uprising; the Bolsheviks did not cancel this measure, for they were obliged, when they first came into power, to appeal to the democratic sympathies of the people.) They thought that this policy would win them the support of the majority of the voters. But they were mistaken, for they received the minority vote at the polls. The Social Revolutionaries, who elected 412 deputies, had the majority. The Bolsheviks obtained only 183 deputies and the Mensheviks 17. Sixteen places were won by Kadets.

Things were made worse for the Bolsheviks because the majority of the Social Revolutionary deputies did not belong to the left wing of this party, which was supporting the Bolsheviks, but to the right wing which was bitterly opposed to them. The Bolsheviks now had to consider ways to free themselves from the Constituent Assembly. In order to strengthen their position they concluded, on November 30, a formal agreement with the left wing Social Revolutionaries. The latter were given several portfolios in the Soviet Cabinet, including that of Agriculture, which was especially important for them in view of their program of agrarian socialism. An elaborate "Law on Socialization of the Land" was approved in order to complete the former Land Decree.

Lenin now felt strong enough to take drastic measures against his political opponents. A strong, ruthless dictatorship was established. The bourgeois newspapers and also the Socialist [with the exception of those supporting the ruling groups] were suspended one after another; political meetings of nonsympathizers were prohibited. A special body of Bolshevik secret police, known as the *Cheka*, was created in order to combat counter-revolution. The Kadet party members were proclaimed "enemies of the people"; their deputies to the Constituent Assembly were arrested and two of them were murdered. The Assembly was finally allowed to meet, but since it declined to recognize the Soviet Government, it was immediately disbanded (January 19, 1918).

THE BREST-LITOVSK PEACE

In December, 1917, the peace parleys were resumed. Since the Allies refused to participate, it was now plainly a question of a separate peace between Germany and Soviet Russia. Germany proposed to the Bolsheviks to apply the principle of "no annexations" first of all to those countries which were formerly "annexed" to Russia, namely, the Baltic countries, Poland and the Ukraine. As to the future fate of those countries, it was intimated that Germany wished to have them under her own control. Thus they would in reality be annexed to Germany. Under the circumstances, there arose an opposition to the peace within the Soviet Government itself. The left wing Social Revolutionaries expressed themselves firmly against the peace and advocated a "revolutionary war." The Communist party itself nearly split on the issue and a group was formed, headed by Bukharin, which sympathized entirely with the Social Revolutionaries in their attitude towards the peace. Lenin continued to advocate the idea of a peace at any price and he was now in the minority even in the Bolshevik Central Committee.

The Government, in view of the possibility of a new

war decided upon the creation of a "Socialist," or "Red" army. This Red army was at first based on the principle of voluntary enrollment.

Trotsky now brought forth a formula "no peace, no war." According to this, the Soviet delegation was to tell the Germans that the war was ended and the old Russian army demobilized; but that no peace treaty would be signed by the Russians. The Soviet Government approved Trotsky's formula and he made his declaration to the Germans at Brest-Litovsk. What the Germans needed, however, was not a mere cessation of hostilities, but the conclusion of a formal peace treaty which would bind Russia for the remainder of the war. Therefore, as soon as the armistice period expired, they started a new advance on Russia. The panic-stricken remnants of the disorganized Russian army fled before them. A few newly-formed detachments of the "Socialist" army could do nothing. Apparently there was no question of continuing the war. Lenin's advice to conclude an immediate peace was now approved by the Central Committee of the Bolshevik party. All the German conditions were accepted and the peace treaty was signed by the Russian delegation at Brest-Litovsk, on March 3, 1918. Russia lost all her Baltic provinces, Poland, the Ukraine, and a part of Trans-Caucasia; in addition, the Soviet Government pledged itself to pay a huge indemnity.

The peace treaty was confirmed by the Seventh Convention of the Bolshevik party, which met in Moscow at the beginning of March. A few days later, an extraordinary Congress of Soviets officially ratified the treaty in spite of the vigorous protest of the left wing Social Revolutionaries. The latter then left the

Cabinet, which became purely Bolshevik, a character which it has retained ever since. Thus the final consolidation of the Bolshevik party government took place. (According to the decision of its Seventh Convention, the Bolshevik party received the new name of Communist Party) At the same time, the site of the Government was moved from Petrograd to Moscow. These were the results of the first phase of the November Revolution.

CHAPTER III

THE CIVIL WAR AND THE SOVIET STATE, 1918-1931

⟨The Revolution of November 1917 differed fundamentally from the March Revolution of the same year. The earlier movement attempted to establish a truly liberal and democratic régime in Russia, but the November Revolution, from its very beginning, was a dictatorship.⟩ By this dictatorship the Bolshevik party under the leadership of Lenin undoubtedly succeeded where Kerensky had failed, but by creating a strong administration that was able to survive in the conditions of general decay and turmoil in which Russia then found herself, Lenin bought success at an enormous price.

The November Revolution destroyed nearly all of the liberal and democratic institutions which the March Revolution had created. In one sense it was a counter-revolution, for it was directed against the régime which had been established by the March Revolution. Judged according to the standards of liberal institutions, moreover, the Bolshevik seizure of power was not only reactionary when compared with Kerensky's régime, but even when compared with the Duma period. Politically, the autocracy of the Communist Party may be compared only with the imperial régime before the Revolution of 1905 and the creation of the Duma. Even before 1905 there had been local self-government, judicial organization, and rights of private property serving as dykes against the inroads of autocracy, but all these things disappeared after the Revolution in November. The Communist dictatorship has been much more ruthless than the imperial autocracy. It has succeeded in holding power by means of terror and with the help of a strong force of cleverly organized secret police. Indeed, the new dictatorship has had an advantage over the imperial régime since it possessed for some time a real dictator in the person of Lenin; the old imperial machine was headed by Nicholas II, a man absolutely unable to play such a rôle.

It is not in the realm of politics, however, that the real meaning of the November Revolution is to be found. It was essentially a social and economic Revolution; it brought different social classes to power, ruthlessly looting and destroying those who had previously been in control. It was quite possibly the greatest social upheaval which history has recorded.

As soon as the Revolution had ended its destruction, and constructive work had been begun, the new Government was obliged to apply methods of harsh discipline not only against the bourgeois class, but against proletarians and peasants as well. The latter resented this bitterly and there were numerous rebellious outbursts against the Bolshevik régime. Even the masses were soon in complete subjection to the very Government which they themselves had hailed so enthusiastically when it was first established.

THE EFFECT OF THE REVOLUTION UPON ECONOMIC AND SOCIAL LIFE

The conclusion of the peace of Brest-Litovsk ended the first phase of the November Revolution and it is perhaps well at this point to consider the first effect of the Revolution upon the economic and social structure of Russia.

The Bolshevik Revolution was primarily a social and economic rather than a political upheaval; its aim was the establishment of an entirely new economic system. Following this program, elaborated by Lenin, the Soviets, during the winter of 1917-1918, decided upon drastic measures against the bourgeois economy. The banks were "nationalized," that is, their funds were seized by the Government. Both domestic and foreign debts of the state were repudiated. Commerce was at first limited and then entirely "nationalized." In the place of commerce, a system of distribution of products through consumers' coöperatives was introduced. Supplies of food and other products were confiscated from stores and private houses. The bourgeoisie were forced to give up their "superfluous" food, clothes, linen, etc. Workers' requisitioning squads constantly raided the bourgeois homes. All food was rationed; it was impossible, except by illegal means, to get bread without bread-cards. A "class-system" was soon established. Factory workers were allowed more food than the civil servants, and the civil servants more than the members of the former "privileged classes." In case of food shortage, the latter could be entirely deprived of their bread-cards. In spite of this system and the fact that the number of soldiers to be fed de-

creased rapidly, the food situation grew worse every
week. This was partly due to the disorganization of
the railroad system, although many other factors also
contributed to the general chaos.

A constantly decreasing industrial production was
one of the most disastrous of these other factors. It is
necessary to note that the factories were not "nationalized" at first. According to the decree issued at the
end of November, 1917, factories and mills were only
subject to "workers' control." The former owners retained ownership but their management was checked
by workers' committees. The result of this dual system was that almost all production stopped. It was not
until the summer of 1918 that the Government decreed
the "nationalization" of the large factories. The small
scale industries were not "nationalized" until 1920.

Meanwhile the "class struggle" which was the chief
political weapon of the Bolsheviks became extremely
acute.) There had been in Russia before the war, as
elsewhere in Europe, a great deal of enmity on the part
of the poorer classes against the bourgeoisie and the
landowners, and these feelings had been intensified by
the hardships of the war period. Lenin succeeded in
capitalizing the situation. This was the easier to do
since this hatred coincided with the enmity of the
illiterate masses against the intelligentsia. The term
bourgeoisie had become almost synonymous with intelligentsia. The result was that not only the bourgeoisie, in the economic meaning of this term, but
every educated man became a target for the indigna-
tion of the mob.

The former upper classes had rapidly lost their social
prestige since the owners of large estates had been de-

prived of their property at one stroke; most of them had migrated to the cities.) Yet the position of the city bourgeoisie and the intelligentsia was not much more pleasant. It is true that in the winter of 1917-1918 the factories had not yet been confiscated, but the so-called worker-control had deprived the former owners of their right to management. New legislation, the "nationalization" of the banks, and the decay of the railroads had destroyed commerce. Many of the former civil servants had lost their positions and all of them had lost their savings. Safe deposit boxes had been opened by Government order and, except for a small percentage reserved for the owners, their contents had been confiscated. Many of the newspapermen had lost their jobs because of the suppression of anti-soviet papers. Because of the abolition of the courts, the lawyers had nothing to do.

In addition, all the members of the intelligentsia had been affected by the measures of the Soviet Government concerning "municipalization" of apartments and furniture. Every bourgeois family was in constant fear of searching squads which, under the pretext of looking for food and fire-arms, "confiscated" everything valuable and arrested or shot the owners if they resisted. The "class-system" of food rationing doomed the bourgeoisie and the intelligentsia to under-nourishment or even starvation.

Thus the bourgeois classes had no reason to be satisfied with the Revolution. The proletariat, or factory workers, had obtained moral satisfaction from the Revolution, but their only material advantage at first was the right to occupy bourgeois apartments. As a matter of fact, it was not the mass of workers, but rather those who were members of the Communist party, who enjoyed this privilege. There was considerable opposition to the Government at the meeting of the Trade-Unions in January, 1918. The Bolsheviks insisted that all labor organizations should at that time be subordinated to the Government, while the Mensheviks had tried to preserve the independence of the unions. The Bolsheviks won, but they only gradually gained the sympathy of the workers. Also, since many factory workers at that time began to migrate to the country in the hope of getting more food, their number began to decrease. The peasants at first had every reason to bless the Revolution, for it had given them land, but their joy was short-lived.

THE CIVIL WAR

In spite of the conclusion of peace with Germany, the economic situation in Russia did not improve, and as the spring of 1918 approached, a real famine began to threaten the large cities. Lenin, at that time, adopted a desperate measure as the only one which could, in his opinion, save the situation. "Workers' food requisitioning squads" were sent to the villages to take grain and other foodstuffs from the peasants by force, in order to supply the cities. A "food crusade" was proclaimed. In order to prevent the resistance of the peasants, the Soviet Government issued a decree establishing "Committees of the Poor" in each village. By this decree the peasant population in each village was divided into two groups; one, consisting of the richer peasants, and the other, of the poorer who were summoned to aid the workers' food squads in their work of taking away grain and other foodstuffs from the richer ones. The poor were promised a certain percentage of the confiscated grain and cattle. The result was an economic *débâcle*. The richer peasants began to hide their grain and to kill and eat their cattle before the poor could report them to the workers' squads.

These Committees of the Poor naturally brought down upon the Government the hatred of the more or less well-to-do peasants and this resulted in a series of peasant uprisings throughout Russia. These purely local uprisings were partly suppressed by the Government with the aid of the poorer peasants. These local difficulties, however, created a very serious situation for the Government, which was fighting against other enemies at the same time—the Social Revolutionaries, the union of the former army officers, and the Cossacks.

The situation was further aggravated by the intervention both of the Germans in South Russia and of the Allies in the North and in Siberia. The Germans occupied the whole of the Ukraine, the Crimea and Trans-Caucasia, and upheld the bourgeois power in all these territories. However, they supported the Communist régime in Russia proper and in Siberia, for they were afraid of Allied intervention.

This was a repercussion of the World War. For some time before and after the Brest-Litovsk peace, the Allies were undecided in their attitude toward the Soviet Government. Although public opinion in Allied countries denounced the Bolshevik as traitors to the common cause, certain individual representatives of the Allies in Russia trusted the sincerity of the revolutionary aims of the Bolsheviks and even hoped to make an agreement with them against the Germans. On the other hand, there was a natural fear that huge stocks of munitions and supplies, sent by the Allies to Russian oceanic ports, would fall into the hands of the Germans.

Gradually, however, the idea developed of ignoring the Soviet Government and of restoring the anti-German front in Russia. The French urged the utilization of the Japanese army to accomplish these aims, but this plan met with the staunch opposition of President Wilson. Although Vladivostok, on the Pacific, was occupied by Allied troops in April, 1918, actual intervention was precipitated by the Czechoslovak legion, which had been formed by the Czech nationals among the former Austrian war prisoners in Russia. Ordered to disarm as it was leaving Russia via Vladivostok after the Brest-Litovsk peace, this force rose against the Soviets, and, with the support of the Social Revolutionaries as well as of the branches of the Army Officers' Union, overthrew the Bolshevik power throughout Eastern Russia and Siberia from the Volga to Vladivostok. An anti-Bolshevik Government was formed in Siberia, which later was controlled by Admiral Kolchak.

At the same time an anti-Bolshevik Government was formed in the Northern Caucasus, which was supported by the Cossacks and by the Volunteer army which had been organized by a patriotic group of officers of the former Russian army under the leadership of General Kornilov. These men regarded the Brest-Litovsk peace as a national humiliation and were attempting to restore Russia's national honor.

The anti-Bolshevik movement in Russia was not a

monarchistic counter-revolution, and its leaders proclaimed their political aim to be the convocation of the National Assembly. But there were, undoubtedly, many individuals among the officers of the anti-Bolshevik, or White armies, who were monarchists. In order to prevent these elements from rallying around the person of the former emperor in case they could have freed him, the Soviet Government ordered the local Soviet in charge of the imprisoned imperial family to kill its members. The whole family was brutally murdered on July 17, 1918.

None of the members of the anti-Bolshevik Government was able to make any close agreement with the peasant leaders, since the peasants were afraid that the Whites would not allow them to keep the land they had seized during the Revolution. The Bolsheviks doubtless did not have the sympathies of the peasants, but they could be reasonably sure at least of their neutrality in any conflict between the Red and White forces.

This war raged for two years, from 1918 to 1920. Both sides were utterly ruthless and the civilian population was subject to great suffering and privations. The Whites arrested and executed those suspected of being Communists, and the Reds practiced the system of "mass terror," arresting members of the middle-class or "rich peasants" and holding them as "hostages" to be shot in case of a subsequent uprising against the Soviet power. According to one of the leaders of the Red Terror, its aim was the extermination of the bourgeoisie as a class. The central *Cheka,* the secret police of the Soviet Government, and its local branches executed in all probability several hundreds of thousands of such "hostages." Military operations often involved the destruction of railway tracks, buildings, bridges, and other equipment. Many cities, in turn, as they became part of the theater of the war, were seriously damaged. In the end the Red armies won, and the remnants of the White armies surrendered or emigrated.

The foreign armies had withdrawn before the final defeat of the Whites. The Germans, on the demand of the Allies, had left South Russia immediately after the Armistice in November, 1918. For a time they were replaced by the French in Odessa and the British in the Caucasus. But after the defeat of the Central Powers public opinion in the Entente states refused to sanction a continuation of military operations in Russia. Allied intervention in Russia was a failure. It had been a half-hearted measure with no definite purpose or plan, not strong enough to be a real menace to the Reds but of sufficient strength to be utilized by them to arouse the patriotic spirit of the Russian people against the invaders.

This was very obvious during the Polish campaign of 1920, which was supported by France and therefore can be considered as the last move of Allied intervention. The causes of the Russo-Polish war of 1920 were rooted in the inveterate suspicions of each nation towards the other. Poland, as it emerged from the World War, had no definite eastern boundary. There was complete political confusion in the western part of the former Russian Empire, for the boundaries that had been established by the Brest-Litovsk treaty became void after the cancellation of this treaty following the Allied victory. The disputes which arose between the Soviet Government and Poland soon resulted in war. Poland was finally victorious and Russia was forced to cede part of her territory,[1] but the struggle had produced and developed a spirit of national patriotism which, of course, followed the lead of the party in power.

THE COMMUNIST INTERNATIONAL

Lenin's victory over the anti-Bolshevik movement was partly due to the rise among the Russian people of a nationalistic spirit opposed to foreign intervention and directed especially against the Poles. By the end of the Civil War, the Red army had become a national Russian army. But neither Lenin nor his associates were Russian chauvinists. Their primary interest was in a world revolution; they regarded Russia only as a drill-ground for the organization of forces for such an enterprise. The staff of this revolution was to be created on the Russian pattern. As the Russian Revolution had been led by the Russian Communist Party, so the world revolution was to be led by a world Communist Party.

This World Communist Party is known under the name of the Communist International. The first Congress of this body gathered in Moscow in March, 1919.

[1] After the close of the World War there was no definite frontier line between Russia and Poland. The Allies suggested the "Curzon line" as the eastern boundary of Poland. This would have given her several districts populated by White Russians and Ukrainians. The actual boundary, drawn after the Soviet-Polish war, was less favorable to Russia. White Russia and the Ukrainian province of Volhynia were divided and Poland received the western part of each district.

It was not, however, until the second Congress of the International that the foundations of the world policies of the Communists were laid. This second Congress met in Petrograd in 1920, and later shifted its sessions to Moscow. At this Congress it was decided that the Communists were to take part in the political institutions of the bourgeoisie, as they called the middle class, or capitalist countries, and to apply *sabotage* methods against them from within. The Communists were also to take part in all parliamentary elections and were to try to elect as many deputies as possible; at the same time they were to attempt to win over the labor unions and other professional organizations. In addition to these open activities, the Communists planned secret illegal organizations in order to prepare for violent revolutions in case parliamentary methods should fail. Communist "cells" were to be organized within the armies and navies of the "capitalist" countries. Special attention was to be paid to the backward countries, known in Communist parlance as "colonial or semi-colonial" countries, as for instance India, Persia, China, and Latin America. Following the Congress, a powerful secret organization of the Communist International was created with headquarters in Moscow and branches all over the world. It was aided by Russian money and by the Soviet secret police, which was first known as *Cheka* and later as G. P. U.[2] The official diplomatic institutions of the Soviet Government abroad, which, as will be seen, spread over the world

[2] In 1922 the Soviet secret police, originally known as *Cheka,* was slightly reorganized and received a new name—that of G. P. U., or State Political Administration. The change was more in name than in fact.

after the establishment of the NEP,[3] were used by both the G. P. U. and the Communist International.

After some unsuccessful attempts to stir up a revolutionary movement in Europe, the leaders of the Communist International directed their efforts toward the Orient. Agents of the International played an important rôle in the Chinese Revolution of 1925 and 1926. In 1927 there was a split between the leading Chinese party of the Kuomingtang and the Communists. The Communists were outlawed and since then they have had to use "underground" methods of propaganda. In the summer of 1930 there was a new outbreak of Communist activities in China.

It was in consequence of the efforts of the Communist International to spread the gospel of the class revolution and communism throughout the world that a great fear swept Western Europe and America. In the so-called capitalist countries the specter of the Bolshevik menace became more terrifying as highly-colored reports of atrocities and destruction spread rapidly abroad. Propaganda of both Whites and Reds, and of their sympathizers, made it very difficult to know what to believe about the Soviet régime. In the hysteria of fear and ignorance which prevailed, even the most unprejudiced observers appeared to be unable to secure exact information.

[3] The NEP, or New Economic Policy, was a compromise with the capitalistic economic principles and was established by Lenin in 1921. See p. 90.

ECONOMIC DECAY AND FAMINE

The Soviet Government was victorious in the military operations of the Civil War of 1918-1920, but the war resulted in the complete destruction of economic life. The system used by the Soviet Government during the Civil War was known as "War Communism." Without a doubt the needs of the Red army were the basis for the whole activity of the Government during the Civil War. The German war system both of industrial mobilization and of rationing the population was the pattern for the Soviet economists. On the other hand, the Communist economic system was not wholly the result of war needs, for it was also an attempt at a practical application of Communist theory; it had been started immediately after the establishment of the Soviet Government and before the Civil War. Nor did this system end with the Civil War. On the contrary, it was still being enforced during the autumn of 1920 after the final victory of the Red army over the Whites.

The Communist system attempted to direct the whole economic life of a huge country from one center. The Government took the initiative in all branches of economic activity and private interest was completely eliminated. All industrial plants were "nationalized," that is, they were managed by Government agents. The land was also "nationalized" and the Government felt free to confiscate grain and other agricultural products in order to feed the city population. Commerce and the banks were "nationalized." The former State Bank, which even before the Revolution had been directly connected with the Ministry of Finance, now became merely an accounting section of the Commissariat of Finance, under the name of "People's Bank." The whole population in the cities and in the country was looked upon as a group of workers in a state enterprise. Decrees on forced labor were issued during the year 1920, for the incentives to private interest had disappeared and it was necessary to provide laborers for the economic activities of the state.

The result was that conditions went from bad to worse. It was only because of the accumulation of wealth before the Revolution that Russia was able to live at all through the years of the Civil War. The output of factories, mills, and mines decreased year by year. Industrial production in 1920 was only thirteen per cent of the 1913 volume. The value of paper money decreased even more rapidly. Worst of all was the situation in regard to agriculture. The peasants, not wishing to work for the Government, ceased to till the land, except to the extent necessary for their own living.

A new series of peasant revolts, reflecting the widespread discontent, broke out in the autumn of 1920. In the spring of 1921 sailors of the Red Navy mutinied in Kronstadt. Under these circumstances, Lenin was obliged to renounce the policy of Communist economy and to reëstablish to a certain degree the bourgeois system. This system, known as the New Economic Policy, or NEP, will be dealt with in the next section. It is necessary now to mention the Great Famine of 1921-1922 which, although it reached its climax after the introduction of the NEP, was really a direct result of the previous system of Communist economy combined with a severe drought which caused the failure of crops in 1920. As both industrial and agricultural production had broken down under the Communist economic system and since the population had been already robbed of its food reserves by the forced food requisitions, the failure of the crops brought on a terrible famine. Some five million persons died either from sheer starvation or its immediate results, in spite of the fact that help came from outside, chiefly from the United States.

THE NEW ECONOMIC POLICY

The NEP was inaugurated in March, 1921, by the establishment of a grain-tax which was to replace the levy of grain. The difference was that the levy system had deprived the farmers of their surplus and the tax meant that the farmer had the right to dispose of the remainder himself. This presupposed the reëstablishment of free markets for staple farm products, which naturally led to the reëstablishment of a commercial turnover within the country. The revival of commerce was impossible without the restoration of banking and money to a sound basis. By 1924 the currency reform was complete and a new stable monetary unit, the *chervonets*, was introduced.[4] The decree on forced labor was revoked upon the reappearance of the usual economic incentives.

The NEP was not, however, a complete restoration of the capitalist economy. The Government kept the "commanding heights" of economic life, that is, the big industrial plants, the railways, a monopoly of

---

[4] One chervonets is equal to ten rubles, or, nominally, $5.15.

foreign trade, and the financial privileges of the State Bank. This economic system was known as "state capitalism." Although private commerce was allowed within the country, the Government tried to check it by operating its own stores and by favoring coöperative trade.

The NEP had a salutary effect upon Russian economic life and there was a rapid increase of output and production in agriculture and in nearly every branch of industry. Towards the year 1928, the industrial output had almost reached the pre-war level and in some branches, as, for example, the production of electrical energy and supplies, it even exceeded that level. Agricultural production, in spite of its progress, still lagged slightly behind the pre-war level.

The introduction of the NEP was followed by the appearance of a new bourgeois class, chiefly private traders, known as nepmen. Many of the farmers reached a level of prosperity unheard of during the fateful years of the Civil War. They were known as "rich peasants" (kulaks). As for the factory workers, their material position undoubtedly improved under the NEP, for their wages were now paid in real money rather than in a depreciated paper currency. But the workers began to lose their commanding position in the state and, for this reason, some of them were not at all enthusiastic about the NEP.

THE NEP IN FOREIGN AFFAIRS

The NEP was something of a compromise between Communism and Capitalism both within Russia and abroad. The Moscow leaders did not discard the idea of a world revolution, but they masked it with the semi-bourgeois face of the Soviet State. The Soviet leaders expressed themselves as anxious to enter the world market as "honest traders," and official Soviet diplomacy tried to keep apart from the "underground" activities of the Communist International. Soviet diplomacy scored its first successes in 1920 by concluding treaties with the Baltic states. The peace with Poland was less favorable. On the whole, the Soviet Government was obliged to confirm some of the territorial losses resulting from the Brest-Litovsk treaty. However, most of the Ukraine remained Soviet territory and the Soviet Government did not recognize the annexation of Bessarabia by Rumania. During the next few years, Soviet Russia made her appearance in world diplomacy and world commerce.

In March, 1921, simultaneously with the beginning of the NEP, a commercial treaty was signed with Great Britain, and, in 1922, the Soviet Government was invited to participate in the conference of the Great Powers at Genoa. No agreement was reached at this conference, but the Soviet Government used the disputes between the former Allies and Germany to her own advantage. A Soviet-German treaty was concluded simultaneously at Rapallo.

The intercourse between the Soviet Union and the "capitalist" world resulted in the *de jure* recognition of the Soviet Government by Great Britain, and later by Italy and France (1924). Other countries followed, and by 1930 it had been recognized by most of the world. As yet, however, the United States has not extended recognition, nor have some of the smaller European countries, as for instance Jugoslavia.

In the meantime, the Soviet Government was busy

attempting to restore the former Russian frontier on the east. It succeeded in recovering a part of the former Russian territory in Trans-Caucasia which had passed to Turkey under the Brest-Litovsk treaty. In 1924 a treaty was signed with China, which recognized in part the Russian claims in Manchuria. In 1925 Japan agreed to evacuate the territory still occupied by her troops in the Russian Far East.

THE SOVIET ADMINISTRATIVE AND JUDICIARY SYSTEM

Although Soviet Russia adopted a constitution as early as July, 1918, it was not until the beginning of the NEP that the Soviet System assumed a really methodical aspect. In 1923 the Soviet State was organized as the Union of Socialist Soviet Republics (U.S.S.R.). The name of Russia was carefully avoided for the idea of the Soviet leaders has always been that the Soviet Union is an embryo of the World Union of Soviet Republics. Any country may join the Union without becoming identified with Russia. The name of Russia was retained for only one of the Republics forming the Soviet Union, that is, for the Russian Socialist Federative Soviet Republic (R.S.F.S.R.). The other republics that were united into the Soviet Union were the Ukrainian, the White-Russian, the Trans-Caucasian, the Turkmen, the Uzbek, and the Tadzhik.[5]

Of course, the Russian Republic now dominates the

[5] The last three republics occupy roughly the former area of Turkestan: the Turkmen Republic corresponds to the western part; the Uzbek Republic to its central part, including the former vassal states of Khiva and Bukhara; the Tadzhik Republic occupies its south-eastern corner.

others, and its capital, Moscow, is also the capital of
the whole Union. If, however, some other large country, such as Germany, should have a Communist Revolution and should join the Union, that country might
perhaps assume the leading rôle in the place of Russia.

The internal political organization of the Union is
built up on the same pattern as that of the individual
republics. There is a Congress of Soviets which os-
tensibly reflects the public opinion of the workers and
peasants throughout the country. There is a Central
Executive Committee, which performs certain parliamentary functions. It consists of two chambers. One,
known as the Council of the Union, is elected by the
Congress. The other, known as the Council of Nationalities, is formed of representatives of single Soviet
republics. The composition of this Council has to be
confirmed by the Congress. There is, further, a joint
Presidium of the Central Executive Committee taken
as a whole. The position of chairman of the Presidium
is comparable to that of the President of France. The
Council of People's Commissars acts as a Cabinet.

The foundation of the Soviet System is based on
local Soviets which exist in every village and town.
Only the poorer peasants and the workers can take
part in the elections. The bourgeoisie, the richer peasants (*kulaks*), the private traders (*nepmen*), and
ministers of the churches are deprived of the right to
vote. Exclusion from the list of voters brings complete civil destitution. Non-voters are denied bread-
cards whenever food rationing is introduced; the co-
operative and state-owned stores will not sell them
anything; their children are not allowed to enter institutions of higher learning and, in fact, are often for-

bidden even elementary education. Aside from the above exceptions, the majority of the population apparently enjoys participation in political life. Even granting this, the Soviet System as it is organized at the present time, is not democratic. The system of Soviets is only the façade of the structure; the foundation is the Communist Party.

The Communist Party is the only party permitted legally to exist in the U.S.S.R. It controls all political action within the country and is so closely identified with the Government that opposition to the party is equivalent to counter-revolution and is vigorously suppressed. Through the political police, the G.P.U., the Communists effectively control all elections and, since there is no secret voting, anyone opposing the program of the Communist Party does so at his peril. The Communist Party is the real ruler of the Soviet Union and the "Politbureau" of the Central Committee of the party is the fountain head of power.

There is no independent judiciary organization. The courts are practically under the control of the Soviets or the Communist Party. The judges can be removed at any time. Moreover, the G.P.U. has a practically unlimited power to interfere with the decisions of the courts and to make arrests without the knowledge of the courts. In addition, the G.P.U. may execute without trial anyone suspected of participating in anti-Soviet activities. The G.P.U. is much more powerful than was the former Police Department of Imperial Russia, for it not only has a much greater network of spies and other secret agents at its disposal, but it has its own troops, which may be utilized by the Govern-

ment to suppress internal disorders when the central
authorities so desire.

THE COMMUNIST PARTY

There are now about two million members of the
Communist Party. In addition, there are about three
million members of the Union of Communist Youth
(*Komsomol*). As regards their "social provenance,"
about sixty per cent come from the proletariat, twenty-
five per cent from the peasantry, and the rest from the
civil servant class and other intellectual groups. The
party members hold all the important positions in the
administration and in industry and trade. The party
every year becomes more and more a huge bureaucratic machine. It has numerous branches all over
the country; each factory, each army detachment, each
administrative office has its own "communistic cell."

The Communist Party is not, however, merely the
ruling political institution of the Soviet Union. It is
much more than that, for it attempts to control the
private as well as the public life of Soviet citizens.
Moral behavior, political opinions, philosophical ideals,
all these the party has settled once and for all for its
members. Every member must believe in a material-
istic philosophy and must be a militant atheist, for
such is the creed of the party. The party itself is
militantly atheistic. Marx and Lenin are its chief
prophets and at the present time Stalin is its Pope.

The ideal aim of the Communist Party is the creation of a social régime in which there shall be no in-
equality and no exploitation of man by man. They
suppose that this aim can be attained by a complete

subordination of the individual to a collective world association of workers. The proletariat, that is, the factory worker class, is the embryo of this future association. That is why the Communists extol the dictatorship of the proletariat as the most progressive form of government. The dictatorship of the proletariat must be ruthless and implacable, since it must face the opposition of all other classes of the nation, and most especially that of the middle class, or bourgeoisie. (The Communists do not doubt the final victory of the proletariat, not only in Russia, but all over the world.) According to them it is as certain to come as was the victory of the bourgeoisie over the aristocracy. To the Communists the whole process of history is nothing if not a class struggle. This struggle, however, will be terminated by the victory of the proletariat all over the world and all class distinctions will then be merged in the true Communistic society. This will constitute the end of history and will produce an earthly paradise. As a matter of fact, the attainment of this ideal seems still to be very remote in Soviet Russia, for class distinctions, as for example between proletarians and *nepmen*, or between *kulaks* and poorer peasants, have become more acute. It is not only the nonproletarian groups, but even the factory workers, if they do not belong to the party, who are deprived of political liberties, and all of the trade unions are subordinated to the party. The dictatorship of the proletariat seems in reality to have become a dictatorship of the party over the proletariat. Far from producing an abundance of supplies, this dictatorship has caused the Russian people to suffer want and even hunger. In 1921 Lenin was obliged to retreat and to establish the NEP. But the Communist doctrinaires were not discouraged by the failure of the first experiment and, in 1928, they started another one.[6]

CULTURAL LIFE UNDER THE SOVIETS

It was quite natural, from the point of view of the Communists, that they should have attempted entirely to subordinate science and the arts to the Communist doctrine, in quite the same way that the Medieval Church tried to subordinate both of them to itself. A number of special Communist colleges and universities were opened and the others were obliged to adapt their schedules to the requirements of the Soviet Government. The same was true of the high schools. Brilliant teachers and scholars were removed or deported if they did not comply with Marxism. As for the students, those of a "proletarian" or "poor peasant" origin are still admitted first, the others being obliged to wait for vacancies; children of the clergy or the *kulak* class are excluded entirely. The Soviet Government has tried to make primary education universal. In this it has failed until now, in spite of very serious efforts. Although universal education was finally decreed in 1930, there are still not enough teachers and school buildings. Some time must still elapse, apparently, before the decree can be enforced.

As for the system of primary and secondary education, the Revolution introduced here marked changes. In the first year of the Soviet Government, the initiative was taken by a circle of pedagogical reformers of

[6] This was the Five-Year Plan (*Piatilyetka*). See below, pp. 103 ff.

idealistic and radical tendencies (non-Bolsheviks), who succeeded in effecting their reform through the Commissariat of Education under Lunacharsky. A decree concerning "A Single Labor School" was published October 16, 1918. According to an explanatory reference appended to the decree, the purpose of the school was to develop in its students a complete and well-developed personality, instead of merely preparing them for some profession. Schools of the "first grade" for children from 8 to 13 years were designed to act as preparation for schools of the "second grade," for students between 13-17 years. These two grades were free and open for all classes of the population. The internal administration of the school was entrusted to the "school collective" composed of both teachers and pupils, with the participation of the school janitors. This system was altered by the decree of December 18, 1923, based entirely upon a "class" principle. It became the purpose of the school to bring up class-conscious proletarians. Education was to be given freely to children of workers and the poorest peasants only. Children of these classes were given preference in the matter of entering school in case of lack of vacancies. Education in the Soviet Union was and is a state monopoly; no private schools are permitted.

In a similar way the Soviet Government managed to subjugate literature. The Soviet Government endeavored to create a "proletarian" and a "peasant" literature, poetry and prose alike. The authorities encouraged the writers to answer in their writings the demands of the "social command" and to write novels in which the personages and the happenings were studied from the point of view of Soviet ideals. However, the Soviet Government succeeded but partially in these undertakings. The tastes of the reader, and particularly of the workingman-reader, do not always correspond to the purposes of the Government. The tastes of the writer, too, do not always and in all respects agree with the demands of a state program. A number of Soviet writers are seeking new forms of literary expression, but many adhere to old traditions. However, one cannot deny that modern Russian literature has many talented authors.

All theaters were taken over by the Government at the beginning of the Revolution and have been run by it ever since. At first there were almost no changes in the program and both Opera and the Ballet continued as before, for the first Commissar of Education, Lunacharsky, was a great admirer of the Ballet. Admission to the theaters was free during the period of War Communism. Since the establishment of the NEP, tickets are required, as before the Revolution, but a certain number of free tickets are distributed among the members of the Communist Party and the Labor Unions. The organization of amateur theatricals among factory workers has been sponsored, and considerable appropriations have also been made for the development of motion pictures. The latter, as well as the broadcasting stations, are entirely controlled by the Government. The Government attempts to use theaters, motion pictures, and the radio for the purposes of propaganda.

The museums were reorganized, and many private collections of art that had not been destroyed during the Civil War were "nationalized"; thus the number of Government museums has increased. The Government tried to establish better facilities for visitors; special guides were appointed to help uneducated people to enjoy the collections.

Much care has been taken to improve the public libraries but all books classed as "counter-revolutionary" were eliminated. The State press has expanded its activities every year. In 1927, 32,644 books were published in Soviet Russia and the total number of printed copies was 221 million. The books were of a different character from those published before the Revolution. Works devoted to the Church and religious problems practically ceased to appear unless they were pamphlets of anti-religious propaganda; the number of these increased rapidly. Almost 45 per cent of the total number of books published were Communist propaganda and tracts. There was also an increase in the number of books on engineering and technical subjects. There is censorship over books and magazine publishing, and newspapers are now published exclusively by the Government and by agencies of the Communist Party. In 1929 there were 611 newspapers in the Soviet Union and the number of daily distributed copies totalled about ten millions.

The situation of the Church and religion in Soviet Russia is very precarious. Theoretically, the Church has been separated from the State, and the Soviet Constitution guaranteed the freedom of religious as well as anti-religious propaganda.[7] Practically, however, the Government has used every possible device to

[7] Since 1929 the Soviet constitution guarantees "the freedom of religious belief as well as the freedom of anti-religious propaganda." The change in wording is apparently an attempt to strengthen the anti-religious drive.

strangle religious life, because the ruling power, the
Communist Party, is a militant atheistic organization.
The properties of all churches, including the church
buildings, have been confiscated, but the local Soviets
were instructed to rent church buildings to religious
associations. Heavy rent and taxes, however, often
make the use of such buildings impossible. Religious
associations are forbidden to take part in any social
activities or to maintain charitable institutions. The
teaching of religion to minors is prohibited. The
clergy are subject to heavy personal taxation and are
denied the right of voting; in many cases they are also
deprived of such elementary rights as the use of the
mails. These restrictions affect not only the Greek
Orthodox Church, but church organizations of all
creeds. However, the Government's policy towards
Islam has been somewhat milder.[8] An "Association of
Militant Godless," with numerous branches all over
the country has been organized and is supported by
the Government. A "Five-Year Plan" to combat religion was elaborated and in it the hope was expressed
that by 1933 no church, mosque, or synagogue would
be left in Russia.

NATIONAL MINORITIES UNDER THE SOVIETS

One of the interesting features of the Soviet System
is the promotion of the national culture of minority
peoples. National minorities are not only given full
political rights but encouraged to develop their culture.
They are guaranteed the unrestricted use of their own

[8] See next section.

language in public schools and in the courts and governmental institutions.   Large appropriations for the press and the schools of national minorities are provided for in both state and local budgets.   Simplified (Romanized) alphabets have been introduced for Oriental peoples to take the place of antiquated Arabic and other Oriental alphabets.   A very important event in the development of the cultural life of the Russian Orient, which resulted from the Revolution, was the political and social emancipation of women; the women of the Caucasus and Turkestan have even been urged to free themselves from the traditional veil.

It is necessary to note, however, that the Soviet Government, although sponsoring the national cultures, requires that they shall be of the same Communist nature as the rest of the Union; all national minorities have to profess themselves strict adherents of the Communist doctrine.   There has been intensive, official, atheistic propaganda in Moslem areas as well as in Christian, but the Soviet Government was obliged to deal much more mildly with Islam than with Christianity, in order not to arouse the active hostility of the Moslem peoples both within and without the Union.

THE RENEWAL OF MILITANT COMMUNISM—THE FIVE-YEAR PLAN

Since no party other than the Communist is allowed in the Soviet Union, political opposition to current policies is possible only within the Communist Party itself.   Lenin had such great authority among the Communists that he was practically dictator of Russia.

But even under Lenin there were attempts at one time
or another to organize factions within the party. After
Lenin's death on January 21, 1924, the personal aspirations of the various leaders accentuated practical and
theoretical differences. Trotsky, Stalin, Kamenev,
Zinoviev, and others, formed different combinations
against each other in order to control the party machine. Among the underlying political motives of the
inter-party struggle, two trends were important. One,
the so-called "right wing" under the leadership of
Rykov, consisted of the men who supported and wished
to extend the NEP. On the other hand, the "left wing,"
whose first spokesman was Trotsky, advocated the
repudiation of the NEP and a return to the policies of
militant Communism. Trotsky was defeated and, late
in the autumn of 1927, was excluded from the party.
In December, 1927, the 15th Convention of the Communist Party confirmed his exclusion and that of many
of his supporters. Trotsky was exiled to Turkestan
and later deported to Turkey.

The fall of Trotsky did not, however, bring the
"right wing" to power. The result was rather the personal dictatorship of Stalin. Stalin had, of course, to
reckon with the fact that many of the factory workers
were dissatisfied with the NEP. Besides, nearly all
of the doctrinaires and theorists of Communism were
opposed to it. They were supported both by young
officers of the Red Army and by the leaders of the
Komsomol (Union of Communist Youth). All of these
groups, although their members were not very numerous in comparison with the peasant masses, were very
active and well-organized. By championing the aspirations of these groups, Stalin seized for himself the

leadership of the "left" Communist group in place of
the defeated Trotsky and defeated the "right." Molotov became his closest associate. At the suggestion of
Stalin and Molotov, the 15th Convention of the Communist Party started a new drive of militant Communism.

The period of the NEP (1921-1928) was, as we have
seen, a period of reconstruction for Russia economically. In 1928 both agricultural and industrial production approached the pre-war level.[9] The economic
attainments of the NEP, however, were accompanied
by social and political phenomena not only undesirable
to the reigning Communist Party, but even dangerous
from the point of view of orthodox communists,
namely, the appearance of a new bourgeoisie in the
cities (*nepmen*) and in the villages (*kulaks*). The
situation in the villages was particularly disquieting
to the Communists. The progress of rural economy in
the conditions of the NEP brought about necessarily
a further growth and strengthening of well-to-do peasantry and this endangered the political dominance of
the Communist Party, considering the purely individ-
ualistic nature of peasant economy. The Communist
Government, therefore, decided to fight the well-to-do
peasantry (*kulaks*).

However, the Communist leaders realized perfectly
that a mere breaking up of *kulak* households would
mean a complete disruption of the economic productivity of the country. Here originated the idea, born
at the time of military communism, of the organization of Soviet farms on a large scale (*Sovkhoz*) as well

[9] See above, p. 91.

as in the form of collective peasant farms (*Kolkhoz*).[10]
The experiment in organizing such farms at the time
of military communism, before the NEP, had been unsuccessful because of a lack of funds and technical
resources at the Government's disposal. Now it was
decided to repeat the experiment on a wider scale. The
organization of large *Sovkhozes* and *Kolkhozes* gave
hope of a simplification of the problem of supplying
the cities with foodstuffs, as well as that of collecting
the grain surplus for the purposes of export. At the
same time, a restoration of the state finances and industry during the time of the NEP permitted the hope
that this time the Government would be able to cope
with this self-imposed task.

The proposed reform of rural economy required a
tremendous increase in the output of agricultural implements, particularly of tractors. But even independent of the needs of agriculture, the Communist leaders
became obsessed by the idea of an immediate increase
of industry. A further growth of industry, necessarily
allied with a growth of the working class, would speed
up the transformation of the Soviet Union into a land
of pure Communism. Important, too, was the question of supplying the needs of the Red Army, that is,
the question of the production of munitions.

[10] The *Sovkhoz* is a large, often gigantic, farm cultivated by
the government with the most scientific and highly-organized
methods. The *Kolkhoz* is also an enormous agricultural area
cultivated, under government direction, by a group of peasant
farmers who have pooled their farms, materials and labor. They
share the produce and profits. By this collective operation, large
scale and therefore more effective and more scientific cultivation
is possible. Restriction on individual profits, and on the tendency
for peasants to become *kulaks,* is thereby made possible.

The result of all these considerations was the springing up of the so-called Five-Year Plan (*Piatilyetka*) for the reconstruction of Soviet Russia and the transformation of the Soviet Union from an agricultural into an industrial country. The idea of the *Piatilyetka* was not, strictly speaking, new. It was merely a resumption of the industrial revolution which had been so vigorously sponsored by Witte in the 'nineties and which had been developing in Russia in the last years before the World War. A new and a very important element in this renewal of the industrialization policy was the fact that the Soviet Government had a far greater power over the country and the population, in both the economic and the political field, than the Imperial Government had ever had during the earlier period. The Soviet Government had no restraints on its activities in the form of the right of private property; generally speaking, the Soviet Government was but very moderately inclined to consider the rights of individuals or even those of whole classes of the population; it was thus enabled to have recourse to such a measure as the extermination of an entire class (*kulaks*).

According to the *Piatilyetka*, it was proposed, in the period 1928-33, to double, and in some departments even to triple, production. It was decided to increase the gross production of industry from 18 billion rubles (at the price levels of 1926-27) to 43 billions for 1933, and the agricultural output from 16 to 25 billion rubles.

This plan necessitated for its realization a huge investment of capital, the construction of a series of industrial establishments, and an extension of the network of railways and highways. There arose also the problem of a new distribution of industry over the territory of the country. Prior to the introduction of the Five-Year Plan, Soviet industry had been supported, to a great extent, by the coal and the metallurgical basin of Southern Russia. In the future, it has been decided to create another such base in the Ural and in Siberia (the Kuznetsky Region). The construction of new factories began not only in European Russia, but in Siberia as well. The more important enterprises, both those projected and those already in the process of construction for 1928, were the following:

Dnieprostroy (a hydro-electrical power plant on the Dnieper rapids); *Traktorstroy* in Stalingrad and in Cheliabinsk; *Autostroy* (an automobile factory in Nizhni-Novgorod); *Selmashstroy* (a factory for agricultural machines and implements) in Rostov-on-the-Don; factories for harvesting machines in Saratov and Novosibirsk; the *Turksib* (a railroad connecting Turkestan with Siberia).

As for agriculture, the attention of the Government was directed mainly to the so-called "Socialistic Sector," i.e., the organization of *Sovkhozes* and *Kolkhozes*, the general acreage of which it was proposed to increase by 1933 to a figure of 60,000,000 acres. In this task of the mechanization of agriculture the main part was to be played by tractors, the annual output of which it was intended to increase to 55,000 in 1933. As the execution of the plan has proceeded, the original requirements have been augmented.

Financially, the Plan required over 64 billion rubles. This sum was to be realized in the following ways: forced taxation; the issue of internal loans; a favorable foreign-trade balance; profits from industry (the latter could be increased artificially as nearly all industry was concentrated in the hands of the Government).

THE ECONOMIC DEVELOPMENT OF SOVIET RUSSIA DURING THE FIRST YEARS OF THE FIVE-YEAR PLAN, 1928-31

The Five-Year Plan was set in motion October 1, 1928. The further chronology of the development of the Plan is somewhat complicated but of considerable importance. The second year of the *Piatilyetka* expired on October 1, 1930. In order to obtain more impressive figures for the results of the first two years of the *Piatilyetka*, the Soviet Government intercalated a "special quarter" and shifted the term of the budget year from October 1 to January 1. Accordingly, the calendar year 1931 became the third year of the *Piatilyetka*. On July 1, 1931, the first half of the third year of the *Piatilyetka* expired, and this was also the end of the first half of the whole Plan. (There had elapsed on this latter date in reality not 30, but 33 months.)

The attainments of Soviet industry during this period are rather impressive. Several large enterprises were completed, such as *Traktorstroy* in Stalingrad, *Selmashstroy* in Rostov-on-the-Don; the *Turksib*. The construction of the *Dnieprostroy* and the *Autostroy* was very much advanced. There was a marked increase in the productivity of many branches of industry. The coal output in 1930 amounted to 47 million metric tons, as compared with 35 in the budget year 1927-28 (the pre-war figure of 1913 was 29 millions). The corresponding figures for petroleum were: 18 million metric tons in 1930, 11 million in 1927-28, and 9 million in 1913. In the field of agriculture one must note a speedy growth of the *Sovkhozes* and the *Kolkhozes*. The crops of 1930 were far above expectations, thus permitting the Soviet Government to resume the export of grain, though the amount exported still remained less than in 1913.

These important achievements of the Soviet Government are, however, limited by several deficiencies. In industry, deterioration in the quality of products has been noticeable in several important branches, such as the textiles. At the same time, the costs of production have not been lowered at all, or at best, not to the level foreseen by the Plan. In several branches of industry, notably in the smelting of pig-iron, there has been a considerable failure to keep the schedule of production. As for agriculture, there was a catastrophic decrease in the number of cattle during the winter 1929-30, a fact which has evidently a close relationship with the policy of enforced collectivization. Thus, after the collectivization drive of the winter 1929-30 the number of horses diminished by 15 per cent, while that of horned cattle decreased by 26 per cent; the number of pigs in 1930 was only 50 per cent of the 1928 figure.

It must be borne in mind that the first draft of the *Piatilyetka* presupposed only a partial and gradual supplanting of the individual peasant economy by collective farming. Later, however, the Soviet Government decided to increase the *tempo* of collectivization. During the fall of 1929 and the winter 1929-30, the process of collectivization went on at a fast pace, being allied with the realization of the program to "exter-

minate the *kulaks* as a class." What occurred during
the winter of 1929-30 cannot be called other than a
new agrarian revolution and it occurred solely because
of an order "from above." Just as in 1917-18 the
estates of the landed gentry had been abolished, so the
households of the *kulaks* were abolished in 1929-30.
The *kulak* land, livestock, and inventory were ex-
propriated in favor of the *Kolkhozes;* the *kulaks*
themselves were not permitted to enter *Kolkhozes,* but
were exiled either to the North of Russia or to Siberia
to the lumber camps. Altogether, several hundreds of
thousands of *kulak* families were subjected to ex-
propriation and exile, affecting in all probability some
2,000,000 persons.

The rest of the peasantry was asked to enter the
Kolkhozes, the entrance being obligatory. Before
joining some *Kolkhoz,* the peasants often killed their
livestock not wishing to give it up to the collective.
This was one of the reasons for the marked decrease
in the number of cattle, to which attention has been
already drawn.

Under the guise of the *Sovkhozes* and the *Kolkhozes*
there sprang to life the system of large estates, abolished in 1917-18. Owing to enforced collectivization, a peasant lost his individual plot of land. Thus,
the peasant seemed to lose all share in the "attainments of the Revolution." It is small wonder that the
enforcement of the collectivization met with open
hostility on the part of the peasants; there were peasant
uprisings in different localities of Russia, especially in
Central Russia, and this spirit of mutiny apparently
became manifest in some parts of the Red Army as
well. Under the pressure of these outbreaks, Stalin

was forced to make an about face. In March, 1930, there was an annulment of obligatory collectivization, and the peasants were given the right to withdraw from the *Kolkhozes*. As a result, masses of peasants left the *Kolkhozes*, especially in Central Russia. On March 1, 1930, the percentage of collectivized peasants had reached the figure of 60 per cent. On May 1, 1930, this figure had dropped to 24 per cent.

A change of policy in respect to the *Kolkhozes* must have appeared to the leaders of the "right opposition," such as Rykov, as the beginning of a new NEP. Actually, however, this was but a temporary political maneuver of Stalin. At the 16th Congress of the Communist Party, in Moscow, July 1930, it was decided to resume an unswerving policy of collectivization.

The heads of the right opposition were forced to renounce their former views. In the fall of 1930, Rykov was removed from his official post as Chairman of the Council of the People's Commissars and Molotov was appointed in his stead. In the winter of 1930-31 a period of increased collectivization began again. The agencies of the Soviet administration, however, did not at this time try to use brute force as freely as before. Thus peasants entering *Kolkhozes* were allowed to retain all or a part of their livestock as private property. Peasant members of *Kolkhozes* were given special preferences over individual farmers; taxes were lowered for them, their cattle were temporarily freed from taxation, and tractors for field work were given only to those peasants who were members of *Kolkhozes*. By the spring of 1931, the percentage of peasants who were members of *Kolkhozes* rose again nearly to the figure shown for March, 1930. (55 per cent.)

The Soviet Government endeavors to make the *Kolkhozes* entirely subject to its authority. A chairman of a *Kolkhoz* is appointed by the Government, and is usually a factory worker. The Government undertakes also the regulation of the mutual relations of members in that most important question of distributing the profits of the *Kolkhoz* among the participants. The former distribution according to the number of members has been abolished and a new distribution according to the number of working days and hours has been introduced; the new distribution is essentially nothing but wages. Practically, the *Kolkhozes* have become simple enterprises of the Soviet Government with salaried workers; in other words, a *Kolkhoz* is gradually approaching a *Sovkhoz*. The main purpose of subordinating the *Kolkhozes* to Soviet authority is the wish of the Government to have a smoothly working system of collecting grain from the population. But despite the seeming success of the *Kolkhoz* growth, the internal organization of the *Kolkhozes* and their work cannot as yet be considered satisfactory.

The Soviet Government faces serious trouble in the field of industry also. The construction of new factories, in spite of some delays, goes on satisfactorily, generally speaking. It seems to be a far more difficult problem to organize normal work in those factories already in operation. The *Traktorstroy* of Stalingrad, the construction of which was completed in July 1930, was not able, even in July 1931, to release the expected

number of tractors.   In looking about for means to
raise the productivity of factories and mills, the Soviet
Government has adopted the system of the so-called
nepryeryvka (uninterrupted work).   According to this
system, factories have to work in three shifts, without
stopping day or night, all the year round (with the
exception of five Soviet holidays yearly).   Individual
workers have one day out of every five, different members of the family often having different days off.[11]

For the purpose of ensuring a faster *tempo* of work
there have been introduced the system of "socialistic
competition" and "shock brigades" (*Udarniki*).   Socialistic competition means competition between different shifts of workers in a given factory, or of different shops in the same factory, or among several
factories working in one given branch of industry.   A
competition may comprise some definite work to be
accomplished or some definite period of time.   The
reward goes to better the living conditions of all the
workers of a shift, guild, or factory.   Besides, the
Government issues individual rewards to workers who
show exceptional efficiency.   This reward consists
either in investing a given worker with the title of
"Labor hero," or in bestowing upon such a worker a
corresponding Soviet decoration or a monetary reward.
The *Udarniki* are special "shock brigades" of the best
workers, who have been commandeered for the "nar-
row stretches of the economic front."   Such troops are
given orders to raise the productivity of some ineffi-
cient factory or mine.   The *Udarniki* get better food

[11] In the autumn of 1931 many Russian industries abandoned
the *nepryeryvka.*

and clothing rations, but in exchange they are supposed to give better and more intensive work.

These means, however, seem not to have raised the efficiency level of Soviet industry. During the winter 1930-31 it became necessary to have recourse to a mobilization of specialists and skilled workers in different branches of industry and agriculture (the mobilization of railroad workers, of agronomes, etc.). The next step was a forced attachment of the workers to the places of their work, and such an attachment has been partially effected. Workers willfully leaving their factories are deprived of the right of obtaining work through the Bureaus of Labor and yet cannot be registered as unemployed.

In spite of all measures directed toward raising production and in spite of an undoubted energy of the leaders of Soviet industry, conditions in the country during the summer of 1931 have continued to remain very strained. The beginning of the *Piatilyetka* brought about a marked impairment in the living conditions of the population as compared with the period of the NEP. The population, with the exception of certain groups, e.g., the *Udarniki*, is but very inadequately supplied with food and clothing. Beginning with the fall of 1929, ration cards have been reintroduced in the cities for food and manufactured products. In spite of the good crops of 1930, there was a shortage of bread in many cities during the winter of 1930-31; the situation in regard to meat and milk products was still worse.

The difficulties in realizing the Five-Year Plan forced Stalin to admit, on June 23, 1931, that some decisive measures for the improvement of the economic life of the country were essential. Stalin pointed out the "uneven character" of the realization of the *Piatilyetka:* some branches of industry march forward at a brisk pace, while others lag behind. In the latter groups Stalin placed such important industries as coal and the metallurgical group, whose inefficiency creates a handicap for the whole Plan.

Stalin admitted that the productivity of labor was still very low and suggested a series of measures which would increase it. In order to make the workers more interested in their work, Stalin recommended the abolition of the leveling system of wages and promised better wages to the skilled workers. Furthermore, he promised to alter the character of the treatment of technicians-specialists, to show them more consideration and to give them better care.[12]

The principle of compulsory labor was not, however, discarded. Stalin openly recognized the necessity of having recourse to conscription of workers from the country, "by means of contracts with the *Kolkhozes.*"

Stalin's speech on June 23, 1931, apparently indicated the desire of the Soviet Government to find a way out of the difficult situation without turning decisively back toward the NEP. At this date (September 1, 1931) it cannot be said with certainty whether Stalin's declaration is a beginning of some serious change in the policies of the Soviet Government, or a mere zigzag, of the same character as the March decree of 1930.

[12] During the winter of 1930-31, those technicians belonging to the old "intelligentsia" were continually accused of counter-revolutionary activities; some were tried for alleged counter-revolutionary conspiracies; others were executed without any trial, on mere suspicion.

Viewed as a whole the Soviet régime has manifest deficiencies. Far-reaching schemes for economic reconstruction have been mutilated by narrowmindedness and fanaticism. The dominant minority requires the absolute submission of the whole nation and is always ready to enforce its own dictatorship with ruthless severity. The individual has been neglected and crushed for the sake of the State. While the Government has sponsored new branches of industry, the average citizen has been deprived of many necessary commodities, and the general standard of living is extremely low. Matters are perhaps not much better "on the spiritual front." The whole nation is at the mercy of Marxian dogmatists. It is possibly not too much to say that in Soviet Russia there is neither liberty of conscience nor freedom in scientific research. Such conditions are hardly favorable for real progress. On the other hand, the Soviet experiment is far from being completed and the time has not yet come to draw up its balance sheet; the final stages of the experiment have obviously not been reached. That there are conspicuous achievements to its credit is undeniable; it is clear that a great nation, in spite of all hardships, is busy at work building up its future.

AUTHOR'S NOTE

THE author wishes to thank his friend, Mr. H. H. Fisher, of Stanford University, who has been kind enough to read the manuscript for this *Study*, for his suggestions as to form and content. The author is also greatly indebted to the Editors for their assistance in preparing the manuscript for the printers and to Mr. M. T. B. Spalding, of Harvard University, who has also read the proofs.

BIBLIOGRAPHICAL NOTE

GENERAL OUTLINES OF RUSSIAN HISTORY

G. Vernadsky: *A History of Russia*, New Haven, 1930 (Revised Edition).

M. Karpovich: *Imperial Russia, 1801-1917*, New York, 1931 (Berkshire Studies).

A. Kornilov: *Modern Russian History*, New York, 1924.

B. Pares: *A History of Russia*, New York, 1928.

S. F. Platonov: *Histoire de la Russie des origines à 1918*, Paris, 1929.

M. N. Pokrovsky: *History of Russia*, New York, 1931. (Marxian point of view.)

D. S. Mirsky: *Russia: A Social History*, London. 1931.

J. Mavor: *An Economic History of Russia*, 2 vols. London, 1914.

CHAPTER I

D. M. Wallace: *Russia*, London, 1912 (Revised edition).

(One of the best accounts of conditions in pre-war Russia, by an Englishman.)

H. W. Williams: *Russia of the Russians*, New York, 1914.

(Good; written by an Englishman familiar with Russian affairs.)

B. Pares: *My Russian Memoirs,* London, 1931.

>(Same; the author was in close relations with most of the liberal leaders.)

Emma C. Ponafidine: *Russia My Home,* Indianapolis, 1931.

>(Personal experience, both before and during the Revolution, of an American who married a Russian and obtained an intimate knowledge of Russian country life.)

G. Vernadsky: *Lenin: Red Dictator,* New Haven, 1931 (Chapter I to IV).

>(A narrative based on Lenin's own writings.)

M. S. Miller: *The Economic Development of Russia, 1905-1914,* London, 1926.

>(A scholarly record with a great many statistics.)

G. Pavlovsky: *Agricultural Russia on the Eve of the Revolution,* London, 1930.

>(A book of the same nature.)

G. Buchanan: *My Mission to Russia,* Boston, 1923.

>(Personal chronicle of Russian events by the British ambassador to Russia.)

M. Paléologue: *An Ambassador's Memoirs,* London, 1923-1925 (3 vols.).

>(Same, by the French Ambassador.)

G. T. Marye: *Nearing the End in Imperial Russia,* New York, 1929.

>(Same, by an American Ambassador.)

S. D. Sazonov: *Fateful Years: 1909-1914,* New York, 1928.

>(Reminiscences of a Russian Minister of Foreign Affairs.)

M. V. Rodzianko: *The Reign of Rasputin: an Empire's Collapse*, London, 1927.

> (Reminiscences of the President of the last Duma.)

A. A. Brusilov: *Mémoires du Général Broussilov: Guerre 1914-1918*, Paris, 1929.

> (Recollections of a prominent Russian army leader.)

W. Churchill: *The Unknown War*, New York, 1931.

> (The Russian front during the World War.)

J. T. Shotwell (General Editor): *Economic and Social History of the World War, Russian Series*, New Haven, 1928-1931.

> (Several volumes; excellent for advanced student.)

CHAPTER II

F. A. Golder, *Documents of Russian History, 1914-17*, New York, 1927.

> (A valuable collection.)

La Chute du Régime Tsariste, Paris, 1927.

> (A valuable collection of documents, in French.)

G. Vernadsky: *Lenin*, Chapter V and VI.

> (See list for Chapter I.)

C. K. Cumming and W. W. Pettit: *Russian-American Relations, March 1917-March 1920, Documents and Papers*, New York, 1920.

> (A valuable collection.)

G. Buchanan: *My Mission to Russia*.

> (See list for Chapter I.)

M. W. Davis: *Open Gates to Russia,* New York, 1920.
    (Recollections of an American eye-witness of the first stage of the Russian Revolution.)

A. F. Kerensky: *The Catastrophe: Kerensky's Own Story of the Russian Revolution,* New York, 1927.
    (A personal chronicle by the Head of the Provisional Government.)

L. Trotsky: *My Life,* New York, 1930.
    (Recollections of a Bolshevik leader.)

A. I. Denikin: *The Russian Turmoil,* London, 1922.
    (Evidence of an army leader.)

S. Oldenbourg: *Le Coup d'état Bolchéviste,* Paris, 1929.
    (A valuable collection of documents in French.)

W. Hard: *Raymond Robins' Own Story,* New York, 1920.
    (Sympathetic to the Bolsheviks.)

J. Reed: *Ten Days that Shook the World,* New York, 1919.
    (Same; a readable account.)

E. Sisson: *One Hundred Red Days,* New Haven, 1931.
    (A readable personal chronicle of the Bolshevik Revolution by a non-sympathizer.)

Emma C. Ponafidine: *Russia My Home,* Indianapolis, 1931.
    (See list for Chapter I.)

CHAPTER III

G. Vernadsky: *Lenin,* Chapter VII to X.
    (See list for Chapter I.)

C. K. Cumming and W. W. Pettit: *Russian-American Relations.*
    (See list for Chapter II.)

L. Trotsky: *My Life*.

>   (See list for Chapter II; Trotsky was the Bol-
shevik War Minister during the Civil War.)

A. I. Denikin: *The White Army*, London, 1930.

>   (An account of the Civil War by an anti-Bol-
shevik leader.)

P. N. Wrangell: *Memoirs of General Wrangell*, New
York, 1930.

>   (Same.)

H. H. Fisher: *The Famine in Soviet Russia*, New
York, 1927.

>   (A detailed account of the American Relief Ad-
ministration work.)

F. A. Golder and L. Hutchinson: *On the Trail of the
Russian Famine*, Stanford University, 1927.

>   (The diary of two travelers in Russia who were
members of the American Relief Administration
staff.)

A. L. P. Dennis: *The Foreign Policies of Soviet Russia*, New York, 1924.

>   (A comprehensive outline of the events up to
1923.)

L. Fischer: *The Soviets in World Affairs*, London,
1930.   Two vols.

>   (The author is sympathetic to the Communist
régime.)

W. R. Batsell: *Soviet Rule in Russia*, New York, 1929.

>   (Outline of the organization of the Soviet State
with many documents translated.)

S. Melgunov: *The Red Terror in Russia*, London,
1926.

>   (A record by a non-sympathizer.)

R. Fülöp-Miller: *The Mind and Face of Bolshevism:*

an Examination of Cultural Life in Soviet Russia,
New York, 1927.

(Good.)

W. H. Chamberlin: *Soviet Russia: A Living Record
and a History*, Boston, 1931 (Revised edition).

(Good.)

J. Douillet: *Moscou sans Voiles*, Paris, 1928.

(The author is a former Belgian consul in South
Russia.)

S. N. Prokopovitch: *The Economic Conditions of
Soviet Russia*, London, 1924.

(A scholarly record of the crisis preceding the
NEP as well as of the beginnings of the NEP.)

A. Baikalov: *In the Land of Communist Dictatorship*,
London, 1930.

(Labor and social conditions in Soviet Russia;
written by a Russian Menshevik.)

C. B. Hoover: *The Economic Life of Soviet Russia*,
New York, 1931.

(A good, scholarly record.)

P. Haensel: *The Economic Policy of Soviet Russia*,
London, 1930.

(Same; the author is unusually well-informed
as he was formerly of the staff of the Financial
Department of the Soviet Government.)

P. Haensel: *Labor Under the Soviets* (in *Foreign Affairs*, April 1931).

(Reliable.)

V. P. Timoshenko: *The New Agricultural Policy of
Soviet Russia* (in *Journal of Farm Economics*,
Vol. XIII, No. 2, April, 1931).

(Reliable.)

The Soviet Union Looks Ahead, New York, 1930.

(An official exposition of the Five-Year Plan, by the State Planning Commission of the U.S.S.R.)

M. Ilin: *New Russia's Primer*, Boston, 1930.

(A readable interpretation of the Five-Year Plan for the students of the Soviet high schools.)

M. Farbman: *Piatilyetka: The Five-Year Plan*, New York, 1931.

(Sympathetic to the experiment.)

B. Hopper: *Pan-Sovietism*, Boston, 1931.

(Individualism *versus* Collectivism as the issue before the World.)

S. N. Harper: *Civic Training in Soviet Russia*, Chicago, 1929.

(A scholarly account.)

A. P. Pinkevitch: *The New Education in the Soviet Republic*, New York, 1929.

(Written by a Soviet educationalist.)

N. Hans and S. Hessen, *Educational Policy in Soviet Russia*, London, 1930.

(Good.)

S. N. Harper: *Making Bolsheviks*, Chicago, 1931.

(Readable.)

W. C. Emhardt: *Religion in Soviet Russia*, Milwaukee, 1929.

(Important for the "Living Church" movement.)

G. P. Fedotoff: *The Russian Church Since the Revolution*, London, 1928.

(Reliable.)

M. Hindus: *Humanity Uprooted*, New York, 1929.

(Readable.)

M. Hindus: *Red Bread*, New York, 1931.

(Readable.)

P. Istrati: *Russia Unveiled*, London, 1931.

    (A rather pessimistic account by a Rumanian author, formerly himself an admirer of the Communist methods.)

A. L. Strong: *Soviet Russia Conquers Wheat*, New York, 1931.

    (Sympathetic to the Soviet régime.)

W. C. White: *These Russians*, New York, 1931.

    (Readable.)

For those who would keep up with current developments the following are suggested: *Current History*, a New York Times Company monthly magazine; Foreign Policy Association fortnightly *Reports* and its weekly *News Bulletin*.

A *Soviet Union Year Book* (A. A. Santalov and L. Segal, compilers and editors) is published yearly in London.

A *Soviet Union Review* is published monthly by the Soviet Union Information Bureau, Washington.

An *Economic Review of the Soviet Union* is published semi-monthly by the Amtorg Trading Corporation, New York.

INDEX

Administration, 10-12, 49, 50, 92, 95

Ægean Sea, 28

Agrarian problem, 51, 52, 66, 71, 89-91, 105, 106, 110-113

Agricultural machinery, 21, 108

Agriculture, 20-22, 32, 52, 60, 61, 71, 89-91, 106, 108, 110-113

Alexander III, 26, 50

Alexandra, Empress, 34, 38

Allies, 29, 31, 41, 42, 47, 48, 70, 72, 81, 82, 84, 92

America. *See* United States of America

Anarchists, 45

Anti-religious propaganda, 101, 102

Army, 12, 29-32, 34, 38, 42, 44, 45, 55, 56, 58, 59, 67, 69, 70, 73. *See also* Red Army, White Army

Army Officers' Union, 81, 82

"Army Order No. 1," 44, 55

Arts, 24, 98

Asia Minor, 31

"Association of Militant Godless," 102

Atheism, 96, 101

Australia, 7

Austria-Hungary, 27-29

Autocracy, 4, 10, 14, 37, 75, 76

Autostroy, 108, 109

Balkans, 27, 28

Ballet, 100

Baltic Provinces, 72, 73. *See also* Baltic States

Baltic Sea, 29

Baltic States, 92

Banks and banking, 18, 19, 63, 77, 79, 88, 91

Belgian investments in Russia, 16

Bermuda, 7

Bessarabia, 92

Black Sea, 28, 29

Bolshevik Party, 57, 58, 68, 72, 73

Bolsheviks, 6, 13, 15, 33, 35, 45-49, 53, 56, 57, 61-72, 81

Bosnia and Herzegovina, 28

Bourgeoisie, 77-79, 97. *See also* Middle Class

Brest-Litovsk, 72, 73, 77, 82, 92, 93

British Empire, 7

British investments in Russia, 16, 19

Broadcasting stations, 100

Buddhists, 24

Bukharin, 72

Bureaucracy, 10, 96

Canada, 7, 25
Carpathian Mountains, 30
Cattle, 110
Caucasus, 103
Censorship, 101
Central Executive Committee of the Soviets, 54, 62, 65, 68, 94, 95
Charlemagne, 28
Cheka, 71, 72, 83, 86. *See also* G. P. U.
Cheliabinsk, 108
Chernov, 48, 52
Chervonets, 90
China, 86, 87, 93
Chinese Revolution, 87
Church and Religion, 24, 25, 51, 101, 102
Civil War, 4, 6, 38, 82-84, 88
Class Struggle, 77, 78, 97
Clergy, 9, 98, 102
Coal, 17, 28, 108-110
Collective Farm. *See Kolkhoz*
Commerce, 19, 32, 77, 90, 91
"Committees of the Poor," 80
Communist International, 85-87, 92
Communist Party, 6, 72, 74, 95-98, 103, 105
Communist Party, Conventions, Seventh, 73, 74; Fifteenth, 104, 105; Sixteenth, 112
Communist universities, 98
Congress of Soviets, 37, 53, 54, 64, 73, 94
Constantinople, 48
Constituent Assembly, 40, 50, 52-54, 70, 72

Constitutional Democrats. *See* Kadets
Coöperatives, 21, 22, 77
Cossacks, 9, 67, 81, 82
Council of Nationalities, 94
Council of People's Commissars, 65, 94
Council of State. *See* Imperial Council
Council of the Union, 94
Courts. *See* Justice
Crimea, 81
Cultural Revolution, 5
Currency, 19, 32, 60, 80, 90
Czechoslovaks, 82

Dictatorship, Communist, 75
Dictatorship of the Proletariat, 97
Dnieper River, 108
Dnieprostroy, 108, 109
Drang nach Osten, 28
Dual Alliance, 27
Dukhobors, 25
Dukhonin, 69
Duma, 11, 15, 18, 23, 26, 33-35, 37-39, 42, 43, 75
Duma Committee, 37, 39

East Prussia, 29, 30
Eastern Orthodox Church, 5, 25, 51, 102
Education, 10, 22-24, 51, 98, 99
Electorate, 11, 12, 49, 94, 95
Emancipation of Serfs, 20
Emigrés, 68
Emperor, prerogatives, 12
Exports, 19, 33, 110

Factory workers, 17, 23, 33, 37, 42, 62, 67, 77
Famine, 89-90
Far East, 26, 93
February Revolution, 37. *See* March Revolution
Finland and Finns, 8, 63
Five-Year Plan, 98, 107-110, 115, 116
Food, 32, 38, 61, 77-80, 115
Food crusade, 80
Food rationing, 38, 63, 77
Food requisitioning squads, 80
Forced labor, 89, 115, 116
Foreign investments, 16, 19
Foreign policy, 25-28, 46-48
Foreign trade, 19
France and the French, 27, 29, 30, 48, 82, 92, 94
French army, 244, 256
French investments in Russia, 16, 19
French loans, 19, 28
French Revolution of 1789, 6
French Revolution of 1848, 6, 43

Galicia, 30
Genoa, 92
German investments in Russia, 16, 19
Germans, 29, 30, 31, 57, 69, 70, 73, 81, 82, 84
Germany, 6, 27, 35, 42, 46, 72, 92, 94
G. P. U., 86, 87, 95
Grain, 28, 61, 81, 88-90, 110
Great Britain, 7, 17, 27, 48, 84, 92

Great Russians, 8
Greek Orthodox Church. *See* Eastern Orthodox Church
Gregorian Calendar, 11
Gregory XIII, Pope, 11
Guchkov, 14, 48

Hague, The, 26
Herzegovina, 28
"Hostages," 83, 84

Imperial Council, 11, 12
Imperial Family, 35, 38, 83
Imperial Government, 4, 14, 25, 26, 30, 42, 51
Imports, 9
India, 7, 86
Industrial Revolution, 5, 6, 15, 18, 107
Industry, 15-17, 30, 32, 60, 78, 88-91, 106-110, 113-116
Inflation, 32, 60
Intelligentsia, 15, 78, 79, 116
International finance, 28
International peace conferences, 26
Intervention, 81, 84
Islam, 102, 103
Italy, 27, 31, 92
Izvestia, 47
Izvolsky, 26

Japan and the Japanese, 19, 26, 29, 30, 82, 93
Jews, 8, 24, 51
Justice, 10-12, 50, 76, 79, 95
Julian Calendar, 11
Julius Cæsar, 11
Jugoslavia and Jugoslavs, 28, 92

Kadets, 15, 27, 34, 49, 56, 71, 72
Kamenev, 65, 68, 104
Kerensky, 15, 43, 46, 48, 49, 55-59, 61, 63, 67-70
Khiva, 93
Khlysty, 25
Kiental, 47
Kolchak, 82
Kolkhoz, 106, 108, 110-113, 116
Komsomol, 96, 104
Kornilov, 57-59, 62, 67, 82
Kronstadt, 56, 89
Krylenko, 69, 70
Kshesinskaya, 45, 57
Kulaks, 91, 94, 97, 98, 105, 107, 111
Kuomingtang, 87
Kuznetsky Region, 108

Labor, 6, 12, 15-18, 33, 60, 79, 80, 114, 115
Land Captains, 10, 12
Land Decree, 65, 66, 71
Latin America, 86
Left Wing Social Revolutionaries, 64, 68, 71-74
Lenin, 4, 13, 15, 18, 33, 36, 46, 62-66, 69, 71-73, 75-77, 85, 87, 89, 96, 97, 103, 104
Leningrad, 36
Liberalism, 4, 37, 38, 43, 57
Liberals, 13, 42, 43, 46, 49, 50, 56, 59
Libraries, 24
Literature, 24, 99, 100
Lithuania and Lithuanians, 8, 30

Local Soviets, 67, 69, 94
London, 60
Lumber camps, 111
Lunacharsky, 99, 100
Lvov, Prince, 39, 40, 49, 57

Manchuria, 93
Manifesto of October 17 (1905), 11
March Revolution, 37, 75
Marx, 13, 43, 96
Marxism, 96
Materialism, 96
Mensheviks, 13, 15, 49, 53, 54, 62, 64, 65, 71, 80
Merchants, 9, 20, 52. *See also Nepmen*
Mesopotamia, 31
Michael, Grand Duke, 40
Middle class, 15, 77-79, 97
Military Revolutionary Committee, 62, 63, 64
Miliukov, 15, 46-48
Mogilev, 38, 58, 59, 69
Molotov, 105, 112
Monarchists, 14, 83
Moscow, 36, 45, 51, 68, 74, 85, 86, 91, 94, 112
Moscow garrison, 68
Moslems, 24
Motion picture houses, 100
Municipalities, 10, 11, 49-51
"Municipalization" of apartments, 66, 67, 79

Natal, 7
National Assembly, 83
National minorities, 5, 102, 103

"Nationalization" of banks, 63, 77, 79, 88

"Nationalization" of factories, 78, 88

Navy, 12, 29, 45, 56, 64. *See also* Red Navy

Near East, 28

NEP, 5, 6, 87, 89-93, 98, 100, 104-106, 112, 115, 116

Nepmen, 91, 94, 97, 105

Nepryeryvka, 114

Neva River, 64

New Economic Policy. *See* NEP

Newspapers, 24, 79, 101

Nicholas II, 26, 38, 40, 50, 76, 83

Nizhni-Novgorod, 108

Nobility, 9, 51

Non-conformists, 5, 25

Northern Caucasus, 82

November Revolution, 37, 74, 76, 77

Novosibirsk, 108

October Revolution. *See* November Revolution

Octobrists, 14, 27

Odessa, 84

Old Ritualists, 25

Opera, 100

Oriental alphabets, 103

Pacific Ocean, 82

Paper money, 60

Paris Commune, 6

Peace Decree, 65

Peasants, 4, 9, 10, 12, 20-23, 51, 66, 80, 81, 89, 111, 112

People's Bank, 89

Persia, 86

Peter the Great, 35

Petrograd, 35-38, 40, 42, 45, 48, 56, 59, 60, 62, 63, 67, 74, 86. *See also* Leningrad

Petrograd garrison, 38, 40, 43, 55, 57, 63, 64

Petrograd Soviet, 39, 53, 62, 64

Petroleum, 28, 110

Petty credit institutions, 19, 21

Piatilyetka, 98, 107, 109, 110, 115, 116

Pig iron, 16, 17, 110

Plekhanov, 13, 15

Poland and Poles, 8, 30, 72, 73, 84, 85, 92

Police, 11, 51

Polish war, 84, 85

"Politbureau," 95

Political parties, 13-15

Political police, 11, 50. *See also Cheka* and G. P. U.

Presidium, 54, 94

Private property, 76

Proletariat. *See* Factory Workers, Labor, Trade Unions

Protestants, 24

Provisional Government, 15, 39-46, 48-52, 54, 55, 57, 62, 64, 68, 70

Prussia, 27

Pskov, 40

Public health, 10

Public libraries, 101

Radio, 100

Railroads, 17, 33, 60, 107

Railway Union, 67, 68

Rapallo, 92

Rasputin, 25, 34, 35

Recognition of the Soviet Government, 92

Red Army, 73, 83-85, 104, 106, 111

Red Guard, 59, 62

Red Navy, 89

Revolution of 1905, 4, 10, 11, 36, 75

"Rich peasants." *See* Kulaks

"Right opposition," 112

Rodzianko, 14

Roman Catholics, 24

Rostov-on-the-Don, 108, 109

R. S. F. S. R., 93

Rumania, 31, 92

Russia, the name of, 93

Russian Empire, Area and Population, 6-9

Russian Socialist Federative Soviet Republic. *See* R. S. F. S. R.

Russo-Japanese War, 19, 29

Rykov, 65, 66, 104, 112

St. Petersburg, 35. *See* Petrograd

Saratov, 108

Sazonov, 26

Schools. *See* Education

Science and Learning, 23, 98

"Shock brigades." *See Udarniki*

Secret ballot, 53, 95

Secret police, 11, 13, 50, 51, 76. *See also Cheka* and G. P. U.

Selmashstroy, 108, 109

Separate peace, 35, 46, 72, 73

Serbia, 28

Siberia, 11, 34, 81, 82, 108, 111

Slavs, 28

Sobor, 51

Social Democrats, 6, 13, 15

Socialism, 6, 39, 43

"Socialistic competition," 114

Socialists, 39, 43, 46-49, 56, 59

Social Revolutionaries, 13, 15, 49, 53, 54, 62, 64, 65, 66, 71, 81, 82

"Socialization of land," 66, 71

Soviet farm. *See Sovkhoz*

Soviet Government, 4, 65, 67-70, 72, 73, 79, 81, 83

Soviet system, 39, 43, 52-55, 94, 95

Soviet Union. *See* U. S. S. R.

Sovkhoz, 105, 106, 108, 110, 113

Stalin, 5, 65, 96, 104, 105, 111, 112, 116

Stalingrad, 108, 109, 113

Standard of living, 117

State Bank, 18, 88, 91

State Capitalism, 91

State Political Administration. *See* G. P. U.

State press, 101

Stolypin, 12, 26, 52

Straits, 28, 48

Switzerland, 47

Tadzhik Socialist Soviet Republic, 93

Tauride Palace, 38

Technical schools, 23

Technicians, 116
Terror, 76, 83
Textiles, 28
Theater, 24, 100
Tractors, 108
Trade Unions, 17, 80
Traktorstroy, 108, 109, 113
Trans-Caucasia, 29, 73, 81, 84, 93
Trans-Caucasian Socialist Federative Soviet Republic, 93
Triple Alliance, 27
Triple Entente, 27
Trotsky, 62, 65, 73, 104, 105
Tsarskoe Selo, 40
Tseretelli, 46, 49
Turkestan, 93, 103, 104, 108
Turkey and Turks, 8, 28, 29, 93, 104
Turkmen Socialist Soviet Republic, 93
Turksib, 108, 109

Udarniki, 114, 115
Ukrainian Socialist Soviet Republic, 93
Ukraine and Ukrainians, 8, 30, 56, 72, 73, 81, 85, 92
Ulianov, 13. *See* Lenin
Union of Communist Youth. *See* Komsomol
"Union of Liberation," 13
"Union of October 17," 14
Union of Socialist Soviet Republics. *See* U. S. S. R.
United States of America, 7, 8, 16, 17, 30, 41, 42, 90, 92
Universities, 23, 98
Ural, 108

U. S. S. R., 93-95
Uzbek Socialist Soviet Republic, 93

Verkhovsky, 61
Village Communes, 9, 10, 52
Vladivostok, 82
Volga River, 82
Volhynia, 85
Volunteer Army, 82

Wages, 18, 33, 60, 116
War aims, 46-48
"War Communism," 88
War Industry Committees, 34
White Army, 83, 84
White Russia and White Russians, 8, 30, 85
White Russian Socialist Soviet Republic, 93
Wilson, President, 82
Winter Palace, 64
Witte, 5, 16, 18, 26, 107
Workers' control, 63, 66, 78
Workers' food requisitioning squads, 80
Workers' and Peasants' Government, 65
Workers' Red Guard, 59
World Revolution, 85, 92
World War, 29-31

Zemsky nachalnik. See Land Captains
Zemstvo, 10, 11, 21, 23, 34, 41, 49-51
Zimmerwald, 47
Zinoviev, 104